Is Atlantis off the South Coast of C

Find out in this revolutionary analysis of Plato's

D0586083

Plato provided nearly 50 physical clues in his famous original account of the story of Atlantis. In this book, author Robert Sarmast cracks the Atlantis mystery wide open by demonstrating how simple facts about the eastern Mediterranean region and the island of Cyprus provide a close match with Plato's detailed narrative.

View Maps of the Underwater Location

Exclusive 3D bathymetric maps based on new scientific data, presented here for the first time, show a stretch of sunken land off Cyprus. The general layout of the landscape of Atlantis as described by Plato is easily discernible in this underwater landmass, as well as the apparent location of its capital—Atlantis City.

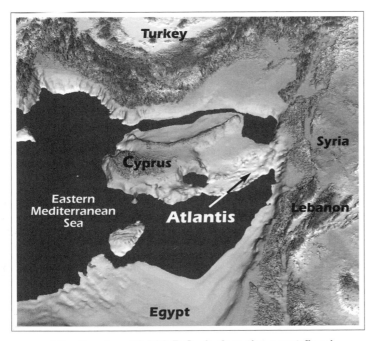

Atlantis circa 10,000 B.C., before the great flood.

Watch Atlantis Come Alive

With the Cyprus location so clearly mapped in this book, the inevitable next step in this exciting and ongoing investigation is a second expedition to the region. Humankind may soon witness the filming of the colossal ruins of this once-mighty empire and proceed to resurrect Atlantis from the deep sea.

Discover the Startling Case for the Island of Cyprus

In this book, the first of a series, author Robert Sarmast joins robust empirical data with other unique findings in ancient history, world mythology, and natural history. Each new fact he marshals makes the case for the island of Cyprus increasingly plausible. With this entirely original theory, Sarmast brings the legendary island of Atlantis alive in a way that will thrill Atlantology fans—or anyone who has ever wondered about the most persistent mystery of the ancient world.

I have virtually no doubt that Robert Sarmast's conclusion...is correct.

—Colin Wilson

Discovery of
Atlantis

The Startling Case for the Island of Cyprus

Discovery of
Atlantis

by

Robert Sarmast

First Source Publications
Tallahassee, Florida

First Source Publications

101 East College Avenue
Tallahassee, FL 32301

Get updates and join the author's email list at:
www.DiscoveryofAtlantis.com

Copyright © 2006 by Robert Sarmast

All rights reserved. No part of this publication may be reproduced,
stored in a retrieval system, or transmitted, in any form or by
any means—electronic, mechanical, photocopying, recording, or
otherwise—without prior written permission from the publisher.

Cover and book design by Phillip Dizick
pdizick@earthlink.net

Publisher's Cataloging-in-Publication

Sarmast, Robert.
    Discovery of Atlantis : the startling case for the
island of Cyprus / by Robert Sarmast
    p. cm.
    Includes bibliographical references and index.
    ISBN 0-9779326-0-5
    (Previously published by Origin Press, ISBN 1-57983-012-9)

    1. Atlantis. 2. Cyprus—Antiquities. 3. Lost
continents. 4. Civilization, Ancient. I. Title.

GN751.S27 2006   0001.94

First published in 2003
Expanded Edition 2006

10 9 8 7 6 5 4 3 2

PRINTED IN THE UNITED STATES OF AMERICA ON RECYCLED PAPER

"For there is nothing hidden
which shall not be made manifest,
nor buried which shall not be raised."

Note to the Reader

The story of Atlantis originates from two famous dialogues of Plato—the *Timaeus* and the *Critias*. Because the argument of this book relies in large part on this source material, we have provided a public-domain translation of excerpts of these dialogues in the Appendix of this book. The reader is encouraged to peruse these important dialogues before reading *Discovery of Atlantis*. Get to know the flow of the dialogues, and look especially for many "factual" references that are sprinkled throughout. We have extracted nearly fifty clues from these dialogues, physical clues that explicitly point to the location and characteristics of Atlantis. This book is built around the author's search for corroborating evidence that matches these clues, as can be found on and near the island of Cyprus.

About the Expanded Edition

Please also note that several sections have been added to the expanded edition. These include: a foreword by Colin Wilson; a new preface by Robert Sarmast; a post-expedition report by Commodore Robert S. Bates; and an insert of eight pages of color images based on the findings of the 2004 underwater expedition.

Contents

Foreword by Colin Wilson xi

Preface to the Second Edition xix

Author's Introduction xxx

1. Plato's Atlantis 1

2. The Universal Myth 15

3. Paradise Lost 29

4. As Above, So Below 50

5. Treasure Hunt 64

6. Secrets of the Mediterranean Sea 95

7. Navel of the Earth 114

8. Discovery of Atlantis 128

    Epilogue 162

    Expedition Report 166

    Acknowledgments 173

    Appendix (the *Timaeus* and the *Critias*) 176

    Notes 188

    Select Bibliography 196

    Picture Credits 200

    Index 202

    About the Author 207

Foreword

by Colin Wilson

I have virtually no doubt that Robert Sarmast's conclusion that Plato's Atlantis was situated in the south part of the island of Cyprus, and now lies under the sea, is correct.

The story of how I reached this rather startling conclusion is as follows:

In August 2004 I received a phone call from a travel agent named Roy Bird, who organizes trips to exotic places. He told me that an American named Robert Sarmast was about to set out on an expedition from Limassol, Cyprus, with the aim of trying to locate Atlantis. He asked me what I thought of the notion that Atlantis might be found in that area. I replied that I could think of nothing less likely. Plato had said that Atlantis was "beyond the Pillars of Hercules," which are generally accepted to be the Straits of Gibraltar. Professor Galanapoulos, the chief advocate of the Santorini theory of Atlantis, argued that two capes of southern Greece, Maleas and Taenarum, were also known as the Pillars of Hercules. But as far as I could see, there was no possible way in which the island of Cyprus, in the extreme eastern Mediterranean, could be "beyond" the Pillars of Hercules on either interpretation.

But, said Roy Bird, according to Sarmast the ends of the Bosphorus were also known as the Pillars of Hercules. And if you were observing these from Greece, you would be looking due east, and Cyprus would indeed be "beyond" them.

I had to admit that if Atlantis was in the Mediterranean, it would explain another puzzle: Plato's assertion that the Atlanteans had been at war with the Athenians. If Atlantis had been somewhere out in the Atlantic Ocean—or even, as my fellow author Rand Flem-Ath had suggested, on the continent of Antarctica—

war between nations so far apart would have been next to impossible.

The reason Roy Bird was ringing me was that he hoped I might interest *The Daily Mail* in the story, and tempt a few hundred tourists to pay cash to join the expedition. I rang a friend on the Mail features staff, who liked the idea and asked me to write an article about it. Which is what I did. However, the newspaper decided not to print the address of my website, which gave details of how potential customers could pay their money. And so, from Roy Bird's point of view, the whole exercise was a waste of time.

But by then I had got hold of Sarmast's book, *The Discovery of Atlantis: The Startling Case for the Island of Cyprus,* and was so intrigued by his theory that I decided to take a holiday in Cyprus with my wife, Joy, and look into it myself. We had a friend who had retired to Limassol—psychic Robert Cracknel—and this would give us an opportunity to go and visit him. He obligingly booked us into a beach hotel in Limassol, and so in September we flew to Larnaca, and were met off the plane by Bob and his wife Jenny. From our hotel we rang Sarmast, who was staying in Limassol, and invited him to dinner the following day.

We had already been told that the expedition would not sail on time, due to various problems to do with obtaining permits. So we did not expect to be able to sail on the ship. In fact, it had begun to look as if it might be months before it set out. But the following evening, when Sarmast arrived at our hotel for an early drink, he told us that things had suddenly improved dramatically and that it now looked as if they would be leaving that weekend.

Sarmast was a good-looking man in his late thirties who was born in Iran but had spent most of his life in America. As we sat on the terrace drinking cold beer, he told me about his background and how he had become interested in Atlantis.

When he left university, he said, he had felt that his priority was to "find himself," and so he bought a one-way ticket to India to avoid the temptation of changing his mind. There he found various gurus, but ended by feeling basically dissatisfied. His story reminded me of so many "religious Outsiders" I have written about – for example, P. D. Ouspensky, who went to India before the First World War in search of a guru who could teach him the meaning of life, but failed to find one until he returned to Russia and met Gurdjieff.

In Robert Sarmast's case the search continued after his return to America. One of the things he came across was a teaching that identified Atlantis with the Biblical Eden. It was in pursuing this odd clue that he came to feel that Eden had been to the west of Syria, in the days when the Mediterranean was far lower than it is today, and when the island of Cyprus had been joined to the mainland.

Like Galanapoulos, he concluded that Plato's figures had been exaggerated by the copyist (even Plato expressed doubts about them), who mistook the symbol for ten for the very similar symbol for a hundred, resulting in size and distance descriptions that were ten times too large. Sarmast went on to point out that:

(1) Plato says that the fertile plain was used by farmers to grow food for the Atlanteans. But such an area is about half the size of England and would certainly provide more food than any city could eat, even London.

(2) Plato says there was a rectangular ditch around the whole plain, into which several rivers were diverted to collect drinking water. But that would provide enough water for ten cities.

(3) Plato says that the plain contained a harbor consisting of concentric circles of canals, all one-hundred feet deep and three-hundred feet wide. But who would want to dig a canal that deep? One hundred feet is the size of five average houses piled on top of one another, and no ship would have that much draught, or even a quarter of it. As to that enormous width, it would accommodate half a dozen aircraft carriers.

So anyone can see that these figures would be more convincing if divided by ten. Besides, said Sarmast, maps show a vast undersea plain twenty-three miles long by thirty-four miles wide. Knock off two noughts from Plato's Atlantis plain and you have these exact dimensions.

He managed to persuade some French oceanographers to let him have a small section of their recent survey of the sea bed covering that area. He found a hill in the exact spot where Plato's Acropolis Hill should have been, as well as what appeared to be a long wall at its foot—again, as Plato described. In fact, as Plato said, the whole hill seemed to be boxed in by walls, as far as one could judge from surveys taken a mile deep.

Later, in the restaurant, Sarmast showed us a computer simulation of the sea breaking through the mountain barrier that once separated Gibraltar from North Africa.

Now it was during the 1960s that geologists first learned that the earth's surface is not a continuous sheet, like the skin of an orange, but consists of tectonic plates which move about separately. Then scientists learned that the Mediterranean is a fairly young sea that was created about seven million years ago, when the plate containing Africa drifted north and collided with Europe. The sea was trapped into a kind of gigantic pond, which extended from Gibraltar to Lebanon. Gradually, this pond evaporated in the hot sun until the floor of the basin was covered with gleaming salt flats.

Geologists have always assumed that the Atlantic began to break through a gap near Gibraltar five million or so years ago, as stated in this book. But since salt beds cannot be carbon dated, no one knows for certain. All we know is that the last great ice age began about a hundred and fifteen thousand years ago, and came to an end about fifteen thousand years ago. We also know there have been many tremendous floods since it ended, as vast northern lakes melted and poured billions of gallons of fresh water into the sea.

Plato, of course, stated that Atlantis was submerged nine thousand years before his own time, which would make it about 9400 BC. Sarmast suggests that about this time, or even thousands of years before it, the shifting of the tectonic plates caused a breach and the Atlantic Ocean broke through what used to be the Gibraltar dam, rushing into the island-dotted salt lake we now call the Mediterranean.

The day after our dinner, Sarmast was having a press conference on board the ship the *Flying Enterprise,* and we were invited —together with Bob and Jenny Cracknell. A television crew interviewed Sarmast on the bridge, and I later did a short televised interview for the local news, explaining why I thought it conceivable that this search for Atlantis, which was being partly financed by the government of Cyprus (mainly for its anticipated effect on the tourist trade), might well produce interesting results. We also looked at the robot camera that could be used to scan at a depth of a mile.

That weekend, Joy and I returned home. In fact, the *Flying Enterprise* failed to leave Limassol the day it was supposed to, apparently still on account of permits. After several weeks I more or less gave up wondering when the expedition would finally set out. But on Sunday, November 14, 2004, Bob Cracknell rang me from Cyprus to say that Sarmast had sailed the previous Monday, and was now back in Limassol, announcing that he had found Atlantis—or something very like it. I lost no time in ringing Sarmast, who told me he had a press conference in an hour but would ring me back later in the day. He kept his promise, and I recorded the conversation.

It seemed that, in spite of initial difficulties, the *Flying Enterprise* had reached the area of the "Acropolis Hill," then released the sonar device on three miles of steel cable, which was towed behind the ship, about fifty feet above the sea bed. Then the winch releasing the cable broke down, and it took a whole night to repair. (This was done by technicians, one of whom had just returned from working on the Titanic.) After another long day making long sweeps over the area of the temple mount, the team went to bed very tired. Robert was awakened with the discouraging news that the generator, which provided the energy for the winch, had failed.

It looked at that point as if the expedition was over, and there was nothing to do but return to Limassol. However, without the winch, the cable could not be wound in. There was only one thing to do—get another generator.

This had to be brought from Limassol, and it was even bigger than the one that had broken down (which was about the size of a small room). And, of course, the ship had to keep moving, otherwise the sonar device would sink down to the seafloor and might well get snagged on some obstacle. So they continued to steam ahead, waiting for the arrival of the ship (the EDT *Ares*) with the new generator.

When this finally happened, both ships had to steer a parallel course while the new generator was transferred to the deck of the *Flying Enterprise* on a steel cable. Sarmast said that he was terrified that, if the cable snapped while the generator was swinging aloft, the expensive sonar equipment would be lost and people would get seriously injured by the flying cable.

Finally, the transfer was made and the new generator installed. The Ares sailed back to Limassol, while the *Flying Enterprise* turned in a huge circle, with its trailing cable, and went back over the mound that they thought to be Plato's Acropolis Hill.

What they were doing, in effect, was using the sonar to "film" long strips of sea bed. But as Sarmast looked at the first results, he was discouraged. They seemed to show very little. When he went to bed that night, he had come to accept that the whole expedition had been a failure and that he was no nearer to proving that the undersea mound was Plato's Acropolis hill.

He awoke to good news. While he had been asleep, the technicians had been working on the long "strips" of map, placing them side by side. And what had finally emerged was a great hill, about three kilometers long, with a plateau on top and unmistakable signs of a great wall surrounding it. He had recognized the signs of a wall at the southern foot of the hill on the original sonar maps provided by the French, but "experts" he had consulted had told him it was probably a mud slide. He had replied that a mud slide that long, and in a straight line, was unlikely, but they had declined to be convinced. Now he had been proved right.

Two weeks later Robert came to London, and he and I appeared together in a television interview about his discovery. While having dinner at Bertorelli, in Soho, I asked him what would happen now. "Now," he said, "we start the long, slow business of raising money for a second expedition with an ROV that can get down there on the sea bed, and see what we've really found."

POSTSCRIPT

In August 2005 the BBC website published a recent discovery that seemed to confirm that Sarmast is correct. The story begins:

> A submerged island that could be the source of the Atlantis myth was hit by a large earthquake and tsunami 12,000 years ago, a geologist has discovered.

It went on:

> Spartel Island now lies 60m under the sea in the Straits of Gibraltar, but some think it once lay above water. The finding adds weight to a hypothesis that the island could have inspired the legend recounted by the philosopher Plato more than 2,000 years ago. Evidence comes from a seafloor survey published in the journal *Geology*.
>
> Marc-Andre Gutscher of the University of Western Brittany in Plouzane, France, found a coarse-grained

sedimentary deposit that is 50-120cm thick and could have been left behind after a tsunami. Dr Gutscher said that the destruction described by Plato is consistent with a great earthquake and tsunami similar to the one that devastated the city of Lisbon in Portugal in 1755, generating waves with heights of up to 10m. The thick 'turbidite' deposit results from sediments that have been shaken up by underwater geological upheavals. It was found to date to around 12,000 years ago—roughly the age indicated by Plato for the destruction of Atlantis, Dr. Gutscher reports in Geology. Spartel Island, in the Gulf of Cadiz, was proposed as a candidate for the origin of the Atlantis legend in 2001 by French geologist Jacques Collma-Girard.

It is "in front of the Pillars of Hercules," or the Straits of Gibraltar, as Plato described...

Sedimentary records reveal that events like the 1755 Lisbon earthquake occur every 1,500 to 2,000 years in the Gulf of Cadiz.

The report concludes:

But the mapping of the island carried out by Dr. Gutscher failed to turn up any man-made structures and also showed that the island was much smaller than previously believed.

This is only to be expected. Spartel Island is too small to have been Plato's Atlantis. But if, in 10,000 BC, it exploded like the island of Santorini eight and a half millennia later, then it would have triggered a tsunami that would have devastated the southern part of the island of Cyprus.

Sarmast understandably regards this event as an extremely powerful piece of evidence for his Cyprus theory of Atlantis.

March 2006

Preface to the Second Edition

When you have eliminated all which is impossible,
then whatever remains, however improbable, must be the truth.

— Sir Arthur Conan Doyle
Sherlock Holmes

I was asked an interesting question a short while ago while being interviewed for an Atlantis documentary: "Why is it important to find Atlantis; why does it matter?" Indeed, why do we, one generation after another, spend so much energy and even risk our lives digging for clues about prehistoric places? The answer is clear: When we look further and further back into our unknown history, we are in reality seeking to salvage the lost lessons of past human experience and gain the wisdom necessary to improve our present condition. An amnesiac could feasibly continue his life without knowing anything about his past, but the recollection of his memory is vital if he is to fully understand himself.

This process of uncovering Atlantis represents my own quest to recollect humanity's lost memory of its origins.

So much has happened since the first edition of this book was published two and a half years ago that it will require another book dedicated to revealing the full account. For just one year after the first publication of *Discovery of Atlantis* we conducted the most scientific Atlantis expedition in history and brought back real sonar evidence showing the world that the target area I had outlined a year earlier was indeed the Acropolis Hill. It has been a remarkable phenomenon that has enthralled everyone involved.

I have learned much since the book's first publication. Perhaps the most surprising part of the learning process, however, has been about a subject that is a major obstacle to every discoverer—human psychology. It is said that people usually believe whatever is in their best interest. Conversely, then, people usually will not believe what is not in their supposed best interest. This is an unfortunate reality which, along with humanity's ever-present-fear of the unknown, has sometimes held back the continuation of my research.

Furthermore, centuries of debate about the Atlantis legend have created a momentum of conjecture about the viability of various theories in the absence of new data—as if we are still unable or not permitted to check our oceans and sea floors.

The old Sufi proverb comes to mind: A group of people are attempting to examine an elephant in a dark room, each taking hold of a different part—a tail, an ear, or a leg. Believing that they had examined the whole, each person thinks an elephant must resemble a rope, a fan or a pillar. Just as the only solution to their problem would be to turn the light on, so must the solution to the Atlantis puzzle be realized by investigating the seas and ocean floors. We are the first generation in history that possesses the technology to do it, so why not use it?

"It is a capital mistake to theorize before one has data"—so said Arthur Conan Doyle's legendary detective, Sherlock Holmes. When it comes to the mystery surrounding the origin of civilization, particularly as that subject pertains to the legend of Atlantis, many educated people simply assume that it never existed without even feeling the need to look first. People are often taught to accept the puerile notion that Plato and Solon, two of history's most profoundly influential characters who dedicated their lives to integrity and knowledge, were just kidding.

But should scientists be expected to give an objective opinion about Atlantis? Science is, after all, strictly limited to tangible and verifiable facts; Atlantis, on the other hand, is a legend based on ancient accounts. Given that there is no physical evidence yet, scientists must necessarily reject the issue until such time as undeniable proof is presented to the scientific community.

Perhaps things would be different if more people were familiar with the beliefs of our distant ancestors. Unfortunately, our universities teach little about the cultures and beliefs of the so-called "prehistoric" races, which is why most skeptics treat Atlantis in isolation and apart from the general context within which it appeared and was understood by the ancients. It takes personal initiative and self-study to see that no matter what ancient civilization one looks at, their religions, sacred scriptures, temple motifs, holidays, ceremonies, rituals, governmental laws, social status and daily lives practically revolved around this legend of the sunken "holy land."

I often refer to Atlantis as the ancient world's "holy land" because that is precisely how the ancients viewed it. Of course, today, the real Holy Land is understood to be the areas in and around Jerusalem where the religions of Moses, Jesus and Mohammad took root. If we think of the period after Moses as being the present chapter of human history, and the period before it as the previous chapter, then a very striking analogy can be drawn: Just as the ancient world practically revolved around the events that transpired in a legendary garden, so do today's religions, scriptures, temple motifs, holidays, ceremonies and daily lives revolve around the events that took shape in the modern Holy Land. Now, let's say that for some reason that modern sacred land was reported to have gone under water never to be seen again; and people living ten thousand years in the future proclaim that it never existed without even so much as looking under the waves to check first. Would that not seem the height of folly?

I truly believe that any honest mind will come to the conclusion that we have indeed found Atlantis once the details and process of discovery are made known. It is all quite logical and founded on elementary deduction.

Based on the enormous and persistent presence of this legend through the ancient world, I formed the hypothesis that Atlantis may have at one time existed, since it would be impossible, at least in my view, for such a monumental and undying legend to have been concocted out of thin air. The testing phase began with the formation of a theory about the likely location of the island and the creation of bathymetric maps which would either validate or eliminate Atlantis as a real place. As reviewed in Chapter 5, a process of elimination was used to narrow the field since "when you have eliminated all which is impossible, then whatever remains, however improbable, must be the truth." Here is a review of the main list of impossibilities which, when removed from the equation, conspire to point us to the eastern Mediterranean as the only logical location where Atlantis could have existed:

1. We are told in Plato's *Critias* that the earthquake which initiated the great flood, and simultaneously submerged Atlantis Island, occurred near Athens in the eastern Mediterranean. It is physically *impossible* for an earthquake in the eastern Mediterranean to submerge an island in the Atlantic some four thousand miles away, much less the Bahamas or farther still. That would be like an earthquake in Los Angeles affecting some area as far as New York or beyond. No one would ever entertain such an idea, but when it comes to Atlantis even serious researchers are found considering places as far as South America and Antarctica. If the earthquake hit the eastern Mediterranean, then Atlantis could have only been submerged if it was also in the Mediterranean. This fact should be enough to point anyone familiar with basic geophysics to turn their gaze solely toward Mediterranean.

2. Atlantis was meticulously described as a striking and mountainous island which rose straight out of the sea and climbed to a great height, having one of the highest peaks known to the ancient world. This means that an island that had mountains rising thousands of feet into the air was almost completely engulfed by the flood. It

is physically *impossible* for the water level of any ocean to suddenly rise thousands of feet! The only way that the towering mountains of Atlantis could have been submerged is if the island was in a very deep basin that was filled up by floodwater, which again points us to the Mediterranean basin and the scientific proof about its massive flooding via the Gibraltar Strait. We know that this tectonic shifting and the resulting flood must have been concomitant with tremendous seismic and volcanic activity throughout the region, which is a precise match with the story of Atlantis's demise.

3. The legend of Atlantis comes from the eastern Mediterranean, not the Bahamas, not the Atlantic, not Bolivia or anywhere else. It was borrowed by the Egyptians from an even earlier race which was literate, probably the Sumerians, and passed on to the Greeks. The Persians, Hebrews, Mesopotamians, and indeed all the peoples of the Near and Middle East had various legends about a doomed island where civilization began and the story was often the cornerstone of their religions. The stories of the gods and goddesses, and the flood itself, had their origin and enjoyed their greatest concentration in the eastern Mediterranean. In my estimation, it is *impossible* for such a cataclysmic event to occur in the Atlantic, the Bahamas or beyond, leave no trace, and then suddenly become the central pillar of culture and civilization for people living thousands of miles away. The legend emanates from the eastern Mediterranean for the simple reason that it all happened in the eastern Mediterranean—the apple does not fall far from the tree.

4. The Egyptians spoke of the art of civilization beginning in Atlantis. Both the Egyptian and Greek civilizations,

and indeed all the great civilizations of the ancient world, were reportedly derived from the archetypal civilization of Atlantis. Bear in mind that it is an accepted fact that everything which marks the beginning of human civilization like reading and writing, agriculture, weaving, pottery, architecture, mathematics, religion and social laws, originated in the vicinity of the eastern Mediterranean. It is physically *impossible* for these arts of civilization to have originated in the Atlantic, the Bahamas and beyond without leaving a trace, and then suddenly reappear thousands of miles away in the Near East. The infancy of human civilization could have only taken place within the area that is the proven cradle of civilization.

These facts, along with other sources that directed me to the eastern Mediterranean, initiated my search for sonar data and led to the consequent map-making process in 1999. Our creation of the underwater maps for the eastern Mediterranean was a necessity since high resolution maps of the Levantine basin did not exist at the time. There were no conclusions to be drawn yet; I was still testing the hypothesis by trying to see if Plato's detailed description of the sunken island could be physically matched with a landmass resting on the seafloor. It did. (See page 1, color insert.)

There was an uncanny match with Plato's description of Atlantis Island: The smooth and flat rectangular valley at its southern foothills, *and* the capital city's Acropolis Hill in the middle of the valley—these were stunning. Indeed, I made over fifty matches, including the flora and fauna, food supply, weather patterns and even the precious metals that are found on Cyprus. Atlantis Island supposedly had unique and striking physical features and the odds that a landmass in the eastern Mediterranean could match the vivid description so flawlessly seemed unlikely to be coincidental.

After publication of these findings in 2003, reviewers from around the world were intrigued by this unique hypothesis which matched not only the island itself, but pointed to the legendary Acropolis Hill as well. But that was only the beginning.

An exact coordinate was provided in the epilogue of the first edition of this book in 2003, against the advice of some of my associates who believed that someone else may beat us to the punch and organize their own expedition.

Plato's description of the size and location of the Acropolis had led me to focus exclusively on this sole target with some confidence. I had investigated it with our proprietary 3D bathymetric models for years even though none of its features could be seen (our maps at the time were not high resolution), and this mountain was too close a match to ignore. (See page 2, color insert, bottom.)

In February of 2004, five months after the release of the first edition, I traveled to Cyprus to see if an expedition could be organized. What was supposed to be a two-month trip turned into a year-long ordeal with a happy ending. In September of 2004, I was greatly encouraged to proceed with the expedition when new evidence confirmed my hypothesis. A French organization (IFREMER) had gathered multi-beam sonar data of our target area and I was fortunate enough to acquire a small part of it, allowing us to finally see the purported Acropolis Hill up-close. New maps and 3D models were immediately created showing the area in detail for the first time, and the results were remarkable. Many specialists who had been critical and skeptical all along suddenly changed their tune and for good reason.

The underwater mountain located at 34.8 N and 35.0 E, which I had pointed to before being able to even see its features, stood out because of several inexplicable anomalies. The features on and around this underwater mountain, and this mountain alone, revealed walls, canals, and river paths that appeared man-made, while all the other submerged mountains in the area were free from any anomalies. (See page 3, color insert.)

As is reviewed in chapter 3, the Acropolis Hill was thoroughly described in Plato's narrative. He reported a flat summit where two rivers originated. These rivers apparently flowed halfway down the mountainside to enter a canal that was dug around the mountain, and then flowed further down to an outer canal at the foothills. The new maps indeed showed just that! The canal wall at the foothills was about thirty-five feet high throughout its two mile course and made a glaring ninety degree turn. Furthermore, this wall was exactly 1.5 miles away from the center of the summit, another exact match with Plato's description.

Aside from the earlier fifty matches with the description of Atlantis, we now had a perfect physical match for the Acropolis Hill. Could it have been merely coincidental that this particular mountain, for which I had provided exact coordinates a year earlier, had turned out to have a flat summit with rivers, canals and walls that perfectly matched the description of the Acropolis Hill, including even its exact dimensions?

The maps and models of the underwater mountain were released to the media shortly after we produced them and the news of the discovery made headlines. The images showed what appeared to be a hillside territory irrigated by canals and protected by massive walls—and they were spectacular. Millions gazed in excitement and sought verification while the "professional skeptics" vainly attempted to explain it as some kind of natural formation. Some said the wall was probably a mudslide, but mudslides do not run in perfectly straight lines for over two miles without leaving trails; nor do they make sharp ninety degree turns. Others said that the anomalies shown by our maps could not possibly be real and were probably caused by errors with the data. One geophysicist even tried to explain the features away as belonging to an underwater volcano, but there is no such thing as a craterless, rectangular volcano. The images spoke for themselves.

The hypothesis that the Mediterranean was last flooded about five million years ago created a lot of justified skepticism. People wondered how our target could be Atlantis if the area has supposedly been under water for millions of years. But the detractors did not know that those time estimations resulted from analysis of core samples taken from an unrelated area. These samples were collected from deeper areas hundreds of miles away from the Cyprus Arc, which is an elevated plateau situated at the northeastern tip of the Mediterranean Sea. The history of the Cyprus Arc is not necessarily related to the seafloor analysis of distant locations, particularly an area as geologically active as the Mediterranean. It has never been "cored," which means that there is no scientific proof available indicating when it was last above water—none! I am quite aware that there were shallow lakes and lagoons in the Mediterranean before the flood, and that they were last dry five million years ago; but what does that have to do with the elevated Cyprus Arc? Until the Cyprus Arc itself is analyzed, the assumption that it also has been submerged for the last five million years is just that—an assumption, not fact.

Additionally, not a single study has ever been conducted to gauge the sinking of the Mediterranean basin despite the obvious fact that the weight of the flood water from the Atlantic Ocean, combined with the effects of tectonic shifting and volcanic eruptions, would force the magma chamber down and lower the basin. Consider also the fact that the esteemed Russian geophysicist, Ya'akov Petrovitch Malovitsky, proposed on the basis of seismic investigations that the Levantine Basin is a "sunken continent."[1]

None of these vital studies have even been factored into the equation, and yet we are expected to assume that the dating for the last flood is final?

Regardless, it was obvious that our own expedition was required to verify the data. Moreover, our side-scan sonar research would give us a much closer look at the wall and the summit itself.

---

[1] Malovitsky, Y. P., Emelyanov, E. M., Kazakov, O. V., Moskalenko, V. N., Osipov, Shimkus, K. M., and Chumakov, I. S., 1975. Geological structure of the Mediterranean sea floor (based on geological and geophysical data). Mar. Geol., 18(4), p. 231-261.

Our plan was to lower the side-scan sonar by cable to "fly" just fifty feet above the seabed so that we would be able to see every detail. (See page 7, color insert.)

We may have executed the world's first and only scientific Atlantis expedition in November of 2004—all others had been simple scuba dive operations at best. It was an enormous challenge, and the work required continues to amaze me. Things would have been so much simpler if only radar could penetrate water; but as it is, searching for objects in the deep sea is still a major challenge today. The entire affair was an unbelievable test of our patience and resolve, and the account of the remarkable stories and adventures along the way will have, as I said, to wait for another book.

After months of processing the sonar data, the images of the seafloor showed what we had suspected all along. The wall is there and it does make a sharp ninety-degree turn, leaving a trail as it moves up toward the summit. It is ruler-straight for over two miles with a consistent height of 35 feet throughout its course. The public release of these images silenced the majority of the skeptics since they clearly show what appear to be man-made structures. (See page 8, color insert.)

When the first edition of this book was released, I could not have anticipated finding such remarkable evidence in such a short time, but now we are close to organizing a second expedition using an ROV to film the wall, move the sediment aside, and at last see what rests under it.

There is no doubt in my mind that we are looking at the oldest man-made structure ever seen by humanity, so old as to make the great pyramids of Egypt seem like modern buildings in comparison. That wall was made by the hands of men.

This research began to test a hypothesis, and has followed the dictates of the scientific process. The elimination of a set of impossibilities pointed me to the eastern Mediterranean, and the bathymetric mapping of the region produced solid results that matched the ancient world's description of Atlantis. Simulation of falling water level was obtained with proprietary software designed for this research, and this effort produced supplementary evidence. The flora and fauna, weather patterns, food supply, etc., to be found on Cyprus also matched. Additional evidence was found with the proof about the Mediterranean flooding. These remarkable correlations stimulated further research with an on-location test using sonar, yielding more results.

All told, an enormous investment of energy, talent and capital to produce these results was made by everyone involved. If at any point along the line some contradictory evidence had surfaced that proved the hypothesis wrong, this research would have ended long ago.

Today the accumulated evidence compels us forward as the Cyprus case warrants more research. Personally, I have more than enough evidence to be convinced that Atlantis has been found, but I recognize that science demands even more evidence. We are close to bringing up the vestiges of the famed island and putting the mystery to an end once and for all.

The greatest discoveries of all are yet to come.

Robert Sarmast
May 2006

Author's Introduction

When Plato first presented the story of Atlantis in two of his most famous dialogues, he may have unwittingly launched one of the greatest mysteries of all time. His vivid story of the origins of civilization on the isle of Atlantis has maintained a grip on the human imagination ever since; indeed, its popularity seems to have increased over time.

Like a persistent echo from the deepest recesses of our collective unconscious, Atlantis continues to flash before our eyes and through our imagination, yet its physical reality has remained hidden in the depths—that is, I believe, until now. Years of work have convinced me that Plato's description of Atlantis was not a figment of his imagination, not just a philosopher's allegory or literary ornament. *Discovery of Atlantis* shows that Plato's richly detailed story referenced something very real: a sunken land-mass, a majestic city, a great people, and a civilization of extreme antiquity.

To actually discover the remains of this magnificent civiliza-tion—all supposedly submerged under the waves of a prehistoric flood—would deal a shattering blow to our present understanding of human history. If Plato's account was indeed in earnest, as I believe it was, then such a discovery may not be far from our reach. Our generation is the first to have the technological means to explore ocean bottoms worldwide in search of the location of this holy grail of underwater archeology—and I have employed some of these scientific tools in my preliminary search. If you read this book and examine the many clues with me, you will easily see how I have been able, step by step, to closely match Plato's story with a specific underwater location.

My claim to have discovered the site of Atlantis, bold as it may be, is not based on casual speculation, nor does it involve awkward theories that trivialize established scientific facts. It is a reasonable, testable hypothesis based on evidence already at hand as well as new evidence especially produced for this work. Writers and researchers in decades past, sincere people who have used Plato's words to pinpoint a favored location for Atlantis, have not had detailed scientific maps to back up their suppositions, nor have they offered theories that do justice to Plato's original account. My hypothesis offers a worthy theory reinforced by science.

The bathymetric maps and three-dimensional models presented in *Discovery of Atlantis* reveal that Atlantis has been sitting right in our midst all along, in the very heart of the ancient world, almost a mile below the surface of the Mediterranean Sea just off the island of Cyprus. In a near-perfect match with Plato's account of Atlantis, these maps hold out the promise and potential of bringing to view the plain of Atlantis, along with the Acropolis Hill, the same "holy mountain" that Plato says once stood at the center of Atlantis City. Present-day Cypriots will discover that their unique legends and folklore that seem to allude to the Atlantis myth were based on fact all along.

Additional evidence, exclusively presented in this book, also points to the likelihood that the legend of Atlantis and the myth of the Garden of Eden are one and the same. I examine this suggestion and offer intriguing evidence that this is indeed the case.

In coming to these conclusions, I closely followed Plato's clues to isolate the eastern Mediterranean as the likely location of Atlantis. I was fortunate to find new underwater data collected about a decade ago through scientific surveys of the eastern Mediterranean, in the area of the so-called Levantine Basin and the Cyprus Arc. The use of this data, in conjunction with specially adapted 3D modeling and animation software, permitted me and my collaborators to chart the area with a degree of topographic resolution far greater than was previously possible. The resulting bathymetric maps published in this book are being presented to the world for the first time. In essence, the application of sonar technology brought us to what we believe must be the location of the archeological remains of the lost civilization of Atlantis, sitting serenely on a sunken strip of land just off the south coast of Cyprus.

As a result of this work, I envision the authentic story of Atlantis moving to captivate the world, with all of its breathtaking beauty and profound implications. That we may be on the verge of a solution to the Atlantis enigma presents us with a potential Copernican revolution in our understanding of human history, myth, and cultural evolution. Humanity has long been mired in a state of mass amnesia about its origins, but through this discovery we will likely be awakened to a vision of a historical and perhaps cosmic reality, the key to which has been lying buried and dormant over the ages under the silt of the Mediterranean Sea. The vindication of Plato is at hand.

In this book I have attempted to clearly present the legend and legacy of Atlantis, acting as storyteller, researcher, sleuth, and explorer. The fields of mythology, history, and geology have all been tapped in order to fashion a vivid and comprehensive image. But in the end it is you, the reader, who must evaluate the research and draw your own conclusions.

Though this knowledge is still relatively new, momentum toward an expedition to the eastern Mediterranean has begun to build through a growing number of individuals who have become interested in its authentication based on the evidence I present in *Discovery of Atlantis*. It is my hope that some who read this book will be drawn to the shores of Cyprus, as open-minded investigators and determined explorers, ready to board the first exploratory vessel, and thus be counted among the courageous and the curious, those working to achieve the discovery of Atlantis.

Robert Sarmast
Los Angeles, California
July 2003

1

Plato's Atlantis

*Then listen, Socrates, to a tale which,
though strange, is certainly true.*

— Plato
Timaeus (370 B.C.)

Few people realize that the philosopher Plato is the sole literary source of the tale of Atlantis. Far from being some New Age obsession, the Atlantis legend was launched by the very founder of Western philosophical tradition. Regardless of how it is mishandled today, this ancient story originally came to us from a noble and distinguished pedigree.

Plato (c. 427-347 B.C.) was a revered Athenian philosopher when he took up the subject of Atlantis toward the end of his career. In two parts of an unfinished trilogy—in the famous dialogues named the *Timaeus* and the *Critias*—Plato gave the world its first glimpse into the remarkable mystery of Atlantis. For some unknown reason he left the project incomplete and moved on to write *Laws,* another great work that was also left unfinished at his death. Nevertheless, Plato's crucial writings about Atlantis—which appear chiefly in the *Critias*—have managed to inspire almost every generation since his time, and in fact remain vital twenty-five centuries later. This is perhaps not surprising, considering that his references to Atlantis appear prominently in the

Figure 1:1
Solon, a renowned Greek lawmaker and philosopher, received the original story of Atlantis from the Egyptians around 600 B.C. This record was passed to Plato many generations later. This relief sculpture is on display in the chamber of the House of Representatives in Washington, D.C.

Figure 1:2
Plato, considered among the greatest philosophers in history, authored the Critias and the Timaeus, two dialogues that are considered the original source texts for the legend of Atlantis and the Atlantean race.

body of work of what many consider to be the most influential Western thinker of all time.

Coming as he did from a prominent family, Plato was lucky enough to have made acquaintance with the leading thinkers and teachers of his time (or any time) including, of course, Socrates and Aristotle. After the trial and tragic execution of Socrates that he describes in his *Phaedo,* Plato declined to follow a political career and instead turned to philosophy in the hope of finding the truest model of an ideal society. No doubt, this philosophical fascination with exemplary social systems eventually led him to elevate the example of Atlantis and its "golden age" civilization in two of his most profound dialogues, the *Timaeus* and the *Critias.*

In these dialogues Plato reveals that another renowned Greek figure named Solon (c. 638-559 B.C.), known to history as one of the "Seven Wise Men" of ancient Greece, imported the story of Atlantis from Egypt. Solon was a truly unique figure, a man of altruistic and poetic temperament, and yet a powerful Athenian political leader and lawmaker. Historians credit him with ending aristocratic control of the government of Athens and, for the first time, introducing a new and more humane code of laws to the city. Solon is widely regarded as one of the founding fathers of the democratic ideal and of the Western concept of the rule of law. To commemorate that fact, a marble relief portrait of Solon stands over the gallery doors of the House of Representatives chamber in the Capitol in Washington, D.C.

It was only natural for Plato to admire and follow in the footsteps of Solon who, like himself, had chosen virtue above profit. The cultural contributions of both men made a permanent impression on Greek civilization and on the subsequent evolution of government in the West. Clearly, the story of Atlantis was promulgated by some of the most remarkable and trustworthy figures of the ancient world.

According to Plato's account in the *Critias,* Solon made a pioneering trip to the city of Sais in Egypt around 600 B.C. He met and conversed with the high priests of the land, taking a keen interest in their claims about Atlantis, among other things.

Plato's narrative about this trip is not a mere legend. Other ancient writers have also documented Solon's historic travels in Egypt, notably the Greek historian Herodotus. In his *History* (440 B.C.), considered the world's first great historical narrative, Herodotus states that the Greek politician decided to travel abroad for a period of ten years after laying down his new code of laws for the city of Athens. But the purpose of his departure was not merely to see the world, as he had publicly claimed; it was, according to Herodotus, a ruse "to avoid being forced to repeal any of the laws which, at the request of the Athenians, he had made for them. Without his sanction the Athenians could not repeal them, as they had bound themselves under a heavy curse to be governed for ten years by the laws which should be imposed on them by Solon."[1] Realizing that his fellow Athenians would need time to adjust to his new and extraordinary laws, Solon purchased a trading vessel and set sail for Egypt.

In those times it was not unusual for philosophers and historians to travel to Egypt in search of knowledge about ancient history. In Solon's day, and for many centuries thereafter, the Egyptians were widely acknowledged as the "most ancient of mankind." They were respected as the best source for information about prehistoric matters. Herodotus himself made a journey to Egypt and spoke with the priests of Heliopolis, Memphis, and Thebes, just to make sure that there were no discrepancies in their various stories about the past. He learned for example that "the Egyptians were the first to discover the solar year, and to portion out its course into twelve parts. They first brought into use the names of the twelve gods, which the Greeks adopted from them; and first erected altars, images, and temples to the gods; and also first engraved upon stone the figures of animals." Like Solon, Herodotus was convinced of the veracity of what he learned in Egypt, saying, "In most of these cases they proved to me that what they said was true."[2] It is not hard to see how a Greek could travel to Egypt to learn about the roots of his own culture and religion—and in the process stumble onto the story of Atlantis.

And so, under the pretext of leisurely world travel, one of the most remarkable legends of all time was able to pass from the Egyptian priests to Solon, who at the time could have hardly realized the full import of what he was learning. These priests unveiled for Solon a detailed and fantastic account of a doomed island that had thrived during a prehistoric era even older than the oldest of Egyptian records. Fascinated with what he heard, Solon returned to Greece with his record of these tales, placing it in his family archives where it remained for over two hundred years.

Plato himself was apparently a distant relative of Solon; this must explain how the story was passed down to him—and may underlie his apparent sense of obligation to pass on this story to his readers not once, but twice, in his writings. By this act of singling out the story of Atlantis and giving it a central place in his work, Plato had unwittingly connected us with the world's oldest and most enduring legend.

Another well-known reference to Solon's sojourn in Egypt appears in Plutarch's *Lives,* including an account of his meeting with the priests of Sais and the revelation about Atlantis. Considered by many to be among the most authoritative and prolific writers of the ancient world, Plutarch—writing in the first century A.D.—refers to Atlantis as "history or fable." This statement reveals the controversial nature of the subject even at the dawn of the Christian era.

According to Plutarch's account, Solon "spent some time in study with Psenophis of Heliopolis, and Sonchis the Saite, the most learned of all the priests; from whom, as Plato says, getting knowledge of the Atlantic story, he put it into a poem, and proposed to bring it to the knowledge of the Greeks. . . . Now Solon, having begun the great work in verse, the history or fable of the Atlantic Island, which he had learned from the wise men in Sais, and thought convenient for the Athenians to know, abandoned it; not, as Plato says, by reason of want of time, but because of his age, and being discouraged at the greatness of the task." Solon undoubtedly spent a great deal of time carefully translating, compiling, and recording what the wise men of Egypt had imparted to his care.

Plutarch then describes how Plato picked up Solon's unfinished work and continued the great task:

> Plato, willing to improve the story of the Atlantic Island, as if it were a fair estate that wanted an heir and came with some title to him, formed, indeed, stately entrances, noble enclosures, large courts, such as

never yet introduced any story, fable, or poetic fiction; but, beginning it late, ended his life before his work; and the reader's regret for the unfinished part is the greater, as the satisfaction he takes in that which is complete is extraordinary. For as the city of Athens left only the temple of Jupiter Olympius unfinished, so Plato, amongst all his excellent works, left this only piece about the Atlantic Island imperfect.[3]

When Plutarch wrote these words, six hundred years had already passed since Solon's trip to Egypt. Evidently, as early as the first century A.D., one of the ancient world's most reliable biographers seems at a loss as to what to make of the legend of Atlantis.

And today's scholars still face the same dilemma.

In the preface to his 1929 translation of the *Critias,* the prominent Plato scholar A. E. Taylor offers a litany of premodern figures who have grappled with the Atlantis mystery:

Strabo the geographer, who disbelieves the story himself, relates (II, 2) that it was credited by the famous Stoic polymath of the first century B.C., Posidonius. Even Pliny (N.H. II, 92) is sceptical. At a later date Ammianus Marcellinus (XVII, 7), the historian and friend of the Emperor Julian, is a believer. The great critic of the third century A.D., Longinus, regarded the whole narrative as a fanciful 'literary ornament'. Many of the Neo-platonists treated it as allegory, though they were not agreed about its interpretation. The less critical among them, Iamblichus, Syrianus and others, took it for history, and Proclus thinks it due to Plato's character for veracity to hold that view....The Middle Ages are said to show no interest in the matter, but the belief was revived in Renaissance times, partly by the rekindling of devotion to Plato, partly by the discovery of America, though the soundest scholars and geographers were mostly incredulous.[4]

Commentaries on the story of Atlantis have come down to us from some of the world's greatest figures, some accepting it at face value, and others—including Aristotle—rejecting it as fiction. To the former group belonged the last major Greek philosopher, Proclus (400 B.C.), who was influential in spreading Neoplatonic ideas throughout the Byzantine, Islamic, and Roman worlds. Proclus believed that the Egyptians did indeed possess the history of Atlantis. He wrote that Crantor, a Greek philosopher and student of Plato—while visiting Sais in Egypt some two hundred years after Solon—was shown a golden pillar inscribed with the history of the sunken isle.

The existence of such pillars was further confirmed by Manetho (c. 300 B.C.), an Egyptian priest who wrote a history of Egypt in Greek. According to this Egyptian chronicler, the history and wisdom of Atlantis was originally inscribed on pillars by Thoth-Hermes, the god whom the Egyptians believed had invented writing, so that the ancient knowledge would not be lost. Intriguingly, Plato's story of Atlantis is in this account traced directly to the prehistoric writings of the "gods" themselves, who did not want their doomed mission to be forgotten in the annals of time.

And it was not forgotten. Regardless of what believers or nonbelievers may think about the reality of Atlantis, the legend always persists. The story has at times been jealously guarded and passed down as if it were truly an epochal event. At other times it has been ridiculed and tossed aside. But this unique legend, almost as old as recorded time, has maintained its vitality and is as popular today as it ever was. Nothing, it seems, can erase Plato's Atlantis from the collective memory of humankind.

At the Festival of the Goddess

The golden age was first; when Man yet new,
no rule but uncorrupted reason knew:
And, with a native bent, did good pursue.
Unforc'd by punishment, un-aw'd by fear,
his words were simple, and his soul sincere;
needless was written law, where none opprest:
The law of Man was written in his breast...

— Ovid
Metamorphoses (1 A.D.)

In both the *Timaeus* and the *Critias,* the ongoing dialogue between Socrates, Critias, Timaeus, and Hermocrates takes place during the so-called Festival of the Goddess. Such festivities were held throughout the ancient Mediterranean world in the pre-Christian era to celebrate and revere the great Mother Goddess, whose divine family was credited with teaching civilization to a primitive human race at some remote time in our ancient past, giving us a quality of life not previously known or even imagined.

Similar renditions of that story formed the essence of what our ancient ancestors, scattered throughout the Western world— even the whole world—celebrated and passed on to their children.

But let us return now to Plato's depiction in the *Critias* of a dialogue that took place during the festival of the goddess in Athens. This philosophic discussion about ideal societies was occurring while in the background the whole community was in a festive mood, busy with all sorts of cultural activities and plenty of good food, good spirit, and good company. It should be remembered that the religious life and national holidays of those early days were largely about giving thanks to nature and its gods, and for celebrating the fertility of the land and its people. These were times when the lifegiving and bountiful gifts of nature were seen as the magic of the gods and the lower spirits who had to be continually appeased by elaborate rituals and bloody sacrifices.

Meanwhile, the philosophers and wise men would gather during such times to share ideas; poets would recite their new poems; and entertainers would dance in the streets. The culturally busy days of the Festival of the Goddess were a natural setting for the philosophers to discuss those legendary times when gods mingled with men, creating an ideal society on a fantastic island named Atlantis. It is plausible that the likes of Socrates, Critias, Timaeus, and Hermocrates would be talking about the heritage and legacy of the goddess on the day of her celebration in Athens.

As Plato now recounts the story of Atlantis—utilizing this special setting as a backdrop—he starts out by telling us how the Egyptian priests at first listened patiently to Solon's Greek version of ancient history. But they were not impressed at all, proclaiming, "Oh Solon, Solon, you Greeks are all children, and there is no such thing as an old Greek." Floods often sweep the Greek cities into the sea, they told Solon, while Egypt has no such worries. Since the Nile River rises slowly and predictably from below, the Egyptians pointed out that they were more capable of preserving and perpetuating the legends of antiquity. The priests further explained that Egypt, not Greece, had the true records of important ancient events, even those regarding the history of Greece, while the Greeks themselves had to start their historic records from scratch after every deluge. Thus, they said, "these genealogies of your own people which you were just recounting are little more than children's stories."[5]

Solon was astonished at this claim; he wanted the priests to tell him more. And this they most certainly did, Plato narrates, citing their belief that both the Greek and Egyptian civilizations were founded and educated by the same goddess. The Greeks had long believed that their own Olympian gods were based on the more ancient deities of Egypt. Solon now learned that the Egyptians, much like the Sumerians, believed that the art of civilization had not been invented by man but was rather imported from the heavens by these gods. The priests revealed to Solon that the records being described to him were passed down for at least nine thousand years in Egypt—making them 11,600 years old to us.

Plato next has the Egyptians describe the physical nature of the Atlantean race and their mighty empire on earth. Although a great deal has been written on this subject by various authors, let us highlight some of the more interesting facets of Plato's account.

The gods had apparently divided the earth between themselves, giving the island of Atlantis to Poseidon, god of the sea. But Plato takes pains to point out the wise and virtuous nature of these gods; he specifically mentions that they did not quarrel among themselves or try to take what did not belong to them. Clearly, these Egyptian descriptions of the gods were rather different from the typically happy-go-lucky and whimsical gods of Greek mythology:

> They retained a certain greatness of mind, and treated the vagaries of fortune and one another with wisdom and forbearance, as they reckoned that qualities of character were far more important than their present prosperity. So they bore the burden of their wealth and possessions lightly, and did not let their high standard of living intoxicate them or make them lose their self control....[6]

These gods descended from the heavens and began to care for the primitive humans that were already on earth. They looked after us, "their creatures and children, as shepherds look after their flocks."[7] But instead of trying to rule primitive humanity by force, this majestic race led by example and kind persuasion; indeed, they were an enlightened race that might be worthy of reverence even today.

But there was more to this powerful and wise race than their role as educators and cultural benefactors of humanity. Just as mortals married and bred children, so too did these benevolent gods. Plato says, "They produced a native race of good men and gave them suitable political arrangements." Amazingly, he goes on to say that these children of the gods later mated with and eventually completely blended with the human race.[8]

Plato is apparently referring to a race that came from the stars with a mission to help civilize our world, causing Desmond Lee, one of the best-known translators of the *Critias,* to call Plato's account of Atlantis "the first essay in science fiction."[9] But of course, this story was genuine history to Plato and his contemporaries. The ancient Greeks believed and taught that they were partially gods themselves, and that they were in fact descended from the gods—and there can be little doubt this belief comes from the same source as Plato's story. And similar beliefs can be found throughout the ancient world.

Aside from their superhuman origin, their extraordinarily developed minds, and their powerful bodies, there is little in Plato's descriptions of the Atlantean race to distinguish them from everyday human beings. Nevertheless, it seems that their mode of living and the laws that governed their society, in Plato's description, were completely different and far superior to any civilization that has ever existed on earth. We might even say that they were initially like a society of industrious and technologically advanced saints, living balanced and nonmaterialistic lives and dwelling in modest homes that were handed down "unchanged to succeeding generations who resembled themselves." Not only did they live modest lives despite their immense power and wealth, but they valued morality above all else—and made it their mission to spread their wisdom and strength throughout the world. Let us listen to Plato again as he relays what the Egyptian priests described to Solon about this remarkable race of gentle giants: "For many generations, so long as the divine element in their nature survived, they obeyed the laws and loved the divine to which they were akin."[10]

According to his account, the Atlanteans were very religious and constructed temples on the most sacred sites of Atlantis. They "loved the divine to which they were akin," since they themselves were descendants of the very gods who had created the laws of the land. Even the great god Poseidon supposedly worshipped a higher power at the most sacred temple on the island.[11] Notably, this most holy of temples is described by Plato as standing on a low mountain in the middle of a rectangular plain. And this was the very place where the earliest generations of Atlanteans were, he says, "conceived and begotten."

The reasons for the destruction of Atlantis may be the strangest part of the whole story. Plato says the high priests of Egypt told Solon that the empire of the Atlanteans continued to grow as long as their high principles and "divine nature" remained unimpaired—for the strength of the empire was apparently correlated with innate wisdom and a superior body and mind. This next passage makes clear the causes of the demise of Atlantis:

> But when the divine element in them became weakened by frequent admixture with mortal stock, and their human traits became predominant, they ceased to be able to carry their prosperity with moderation.[12]

In other words, the heroic Atlanteans, originally born of the immortal gods and vehicles of their superior DNA, lost their genetic superiority by "frequent admixture with mortal stock." Tragically, they slowly sank to the level of primitive and often savage humans. And as their conquests of neighboring people became ever more ambitious, so too did their reign slowly become tyrannical. Soon the "degeneration" of their once noble race became obvious to all, Plato indicates. They began to hate each other and fell to the abysmal level of fighting amongst themselves for earthly rewards. It was at this time that Zeus decided to "reduce them" by punishment—and Atlantis was suddenly destroyed by earthquake and flood:

And the god of gods, Zeus, who reigns by law, and
whose eye can see such things, when he perceived
the wretched state of this admirable stock decided to
punish them and reduce them to order by discipline.[13]

Very few contemporary researchers focus on this genetic degrada-
tion of the Atlanteans, but Plato is explicit in this regard and leaves
little to imagination. It is clear that the ancient Greeks, like their
Egyptian counterparts, believed in the sacred and immortal blood
of these gods, which the Greeks called the *Ichor.*

Before we move on to consider the physical layout of Atlantis
Island, let us pause to review what Plato has told us about the
Atlantean race thus far. The Atlanteans were a race of superhuman
beings that were the descendants of Poseidon, god of the sea.
They had been allotted the island of Atlantis, but soon the family
of this unique race grew in numbers and ambition. Eventually,
they branched out to the neighboring areas where they ruled the
masses with wisdom and care. Under the benevolent care of this
godlike race the indigenous peoples in the surrounding lands
learned about civilization for the first time and began to practice
agriculture, architecture, the arts, industry, and religion. So long
as the Atlanteans maintained their blood pure and ruled by the
altruistic laws of the high gods, their empire grew and brought
fortune to themselves and all their subjects. But in time they began
to mate with the natives and subsequently lost their special
genetic disposition until they eventually became more like
ordinary humans: hungry for power and domination. Zeus then
decided to punish them by destroying their home with a massive
flood and earthquake, thus destroying Atlantis and all its wicked
inhabitants.

Figure 1:3
Poseidon, god of the sea.
This painting of Poseidon and Venus by the artist Brumidi was commissioned by Thomas Jefferson in the late 18th century and can be seen in the rotunda of the Capitol in Washington, D.C. Plato indicates that the gods allotted the island of Atlantis to Poseidon, whose offspring became the mighty Atlantean race.

2

The Universal Myth

Of Man's first disobedience, and the fruit
of that forbidden tree, whose mortal taste
brought death into the world, and all our woe,
with loss of Eden, till one greater Man
restore us, and regain the blissful seat.

— Milton
Paradise Lost (1667)

There is no story more ancient and pervasive than the legend about a group of wise and powerful gods who descended to earth and taught civilization to humankind. It was once believed that these earthbound gods procreated amongst themselves, producing a mighty race of giants that went on to teach the art of civilization to the indigenous men of earth. Even from the time that humanity first began to record history on clay tablets, or inscribe their beliefs on stone, the story of the "pure land" was already well established and considered a real event that transpired in prehistoric times. From Mesopotamia to Egypt to Greece and to India and beyond, the oldest records unearthed by archeologists reveal the existence of a near-universal belief in the descent of the gods to earth.

We have already considered some of the important similarities between the legend of Atlantis and these older myths of a prehistoric golden age. These primeval stories of the origins of civilization are so eerily similar and so widespread in ancient myth that they seem to blend into what I have called a "universal myth." General ignorance of this legacy of humankind, however, has caused many writers to view the Atlantis story in isolation, apart from the wider context of world mythology prevalent in Plato's time. If we are to understand how Plato's generation may have viewed his tale of Atlantis, we would need to understand this universal story of the mystery gods and the grip it held on his contemporaries, and on later writers in the Mediterranean world. In other words, the ancients accepted and perpetuated the story of Atlantis primarily because it harmonized with their accepted understanding of human origins, not just because Plato may have written about it in a philosophical dialogue.

In our time, comparative mythologists have often remarked that these ancient stories, even those from different continents, seem strangely similar. The most common explanation from modern scholars relies on depth psychology—the convenient notion that the human psyche creates these kinds of legends in order to satisfy an instinctive desire for myths and heroes. According to Carl Jung, "myths are original revelations of the pre-conscious psyche, involuntary statements about unconscious happenings."[1] Joseph Campbell, heavily influenced by Jung, proposed the popular theory that all myths are linked in the human psyche, showing up in particular cultures as archetypal manifestations of humanity's deeply felt need to explain social, cosmological, and spiritual realities. But are we to believe that different cultures, when completely isolated from one another, will always come up with the same basic legend?

Ancient peoples believed that wise gods had fallen from faraway stars; some societies even point to distinct areas of space, such as the Pleiades, as the place from which they fell. Are we also to believe that odd details like these, which appear in the records of diverse cultures, are nothing more than projections of the human psyche?

One vivid example is that of the myth of the goddess Ashtart (Ishtar), who was worshipped in many coastal cities of the eastern Mediterranean. Ashtart supposedly fell from heaven as "an egg of wondrous size." This old myth was later absorbed by the Christians, who celebrate Easter on Ishtar's birthday—and in fact named the holiday after her. Today's colored Easter eggs once symbolized the "wondrous egg" that fell from heaven, carrying the goddess inside. In *The Two Babylons,* Alexander Hislop writes:

> The classic poets are full of the fable of the mystic egg of the Babylonians; and thus its tale is told by Hyginus, the Egyptian, the learned keeper of the Palatine library at Rome, in the time of Augustus, who was skilled in all the wisdom of his native country: 'An egg of wondrous size is said to have fallen from heaven into the river Euphrates. The fishes rolled it to the bank, where the doves having settled upon it, and hatched it, out came Venus, who afterwards was called the Syrian Goddess'—that is, *Astarte.* Hence the egg became one of the symbols of Astarte or Easter; and accordingly, in Cyprus, one of the chosen seats of the worship of Venus, or Astarte, the egg of wondrous size was represented on a grand scale.[2]

As Hislop indicates, Cyprus became a seat of her worship. Her mystery was so powerful that the word "star" is itself derived from the Babylonian "Ishtar."[3]

Let us consider more stories of gods or goddesses who fell to earth. In the New Testament (Acts 19:35) we read that Apostle Paul was rejected by the Ephesians as the angry masses chanted the name of the goddess Diana, who had "fallen down from Jupiter." Diana was in turn modeled on the Ephesian goddess of fertility and sexuality, Artemis, the most ancient sculpture of whom was cut from a black meteorite called the "sacred stone."[4] Likewise, before the Islamic prophet Muhammad abolished idol worship in Arabia, a sacred stone was kept in the holy shrine of Al'Lat, the Arabian version of the great goddess. This stone was said to be a black meteorite that, as in the stories of Ishtar and Diana, had fallen from heaven and was therefore identified with the other-worldly nature of the goddess.

Predating these myths are the Sumerian story of Father Enki, the Egyptian legend of Isis and Osiris, and the Persian belief in Mithra—gods who also came down from above and mingled with men.

Whether we look at the legends of the Sumerians, Egyptians, Persians, or later ones of the Greeks or Romans, we find the mystery gods at the center of each culture, affecting every facet of civilization including holidays, religious beliefs, governmental laws, social etiquette, and architectural designs. Kings and queens of many of the world's ancient empires traced their so-called divine lineage back to these same gods; soldiers fought in their name, and the masses worshipped them through daily rituals and sacrifice. As with the Atlantean gods, the Sumerian gods (or at least those who descended to earth and mingled with men) were in many ways similar to humans. In *The Sumerians: Their History, Culture and Character* (1963), Samuel Noah Kramer writes:

> The Sumerian gods, as illustrated graphically by the Sumerian myths, were entirely anthropomorphic; even the most powerful and most knowing among them were conceived as human in form, thought, and deed. Like man, they plan and act, eat and drink, marry and raise families, support large households, and are addicted to human passions and weaknesses. By and large they prefer truth and justice to falsehood and oppression, but their motives are by no means clear, and man is often at a loss to understand them.[5]

Like the Greeks, the Sumerians attributed all of their might and majesty to the knowledge and wisdom imparted to them by the gods, and more importantly, to the inheritance of their sacred blood. This "immortal" bloodline was thought to be responsible for their cultural superiority and was vigorously guarded in the royal line of all their rulers.

As noted by writers such as Zecharia Sitchin, unearthed clay tablets show that over five thousand years ago the Sumerians were religiously teaching the impact of the visiting gods on their culture. The Sumerians believed the gods had interbred with humans, just as Plato's *Critias* claimed that Atlanteans had mated with mortals. In the famed *Gilgamesh Epic,* the hero Gilgamesh is described as being two-thirds god and one-third man. In the Sumerian *Atrahasis,* a creation story dating to at least 1700 B.C., we read that the gods intentionally mixed their own bloodline with that of humans, so that "a god and a man will be mixed together in clay."[6]

Like the story of Poseidon and the Atlantean race, the Sumerian Father Enki and other ranking gods and goddesses are said to have descended from Paradise. They taught the skills of civilization to humankind, instructing people on the art of living through technology, organization, and the proper worship of the celestial gods. Like Poseidon in Atlantis, Enki proceeded to form an empire, create a family of mighty offspring, and build temples for his celestial father, "the king of heaven and earth."

A most remarkable collection of tablets dating back to the third millennium B.C., aptly named *Enki and the World Order,* describes the story in detail, as summarized by Thorkild Jacobsen in his classic work *Treasures of Darkness* (1976):

> In the myth called 'Enki and the World Order' we hear how Enki organized the cosmos for Enlil in just such terms. He instituted the regime of the Euphrates and the Tigris, appointed the god Enbilulu as divine 'inspector of canals', and he arranged the marshes and the sea, appointing divine officials to take charge of them. Next he organized the rains and put Ishkur in charge. There followed the instituting of agriculture: ploughing, irrigation, and harvesting, the appointment of the farmer god Enkimdu and the grain goddess, Ezinu. After agriculture came brickmaking and the builder's craft under the brick god, Kulla, and the

divine architect, Mushdama; and in similar manner Enki organized the wild life of the desert, founded husbandry, fixed boundaries, set limits for building plots and fields, and instituted weaving—in each case appointing appropriate gods to the offices of supervision.[7]

These beliefs are especially interesting in light of the fact that the Sumerians were exceedingly advanced for their time and seemed to appear on the world stage from out of nowhere. In *The Masks of God* (1959), Joseph Campbell wrote: "With stunning abruptness . . . there appears in this little Sumerian mud garden ... the whole cultural syndrome that has since constituted the germinal unit of all the high civilizations of the world." Without a trace of origin, the Sumerian people appear in the annals of history complete with a fully developed culture—the rule of law, a sophisticated religion, skilled agriculture, advanced architecture, metal-working, temples and libraries, writing and publishing, mathematics, astronomy, calendars, pottery, and weaving—all at a time when the rest of the world was still living at a markedly primitive level.

The Egyptians, as well, were adamant in their belief in a prehistoric era in which certain gods descended from the stars and gave civilization to mankind. This is clearly stated in Plato's *Critias,* which had its source in Egypt, but other Egyptian legends also tell this story. It was commonly believed that Osiris, along with his wife Isis, had descended from the stars to help humankind. They were similar to humans in form and gave birth to a race of superior beings right here on earth, just like the Atlanteans. E. A. Wallis Budge, the renowned early Egyptologist, writing about the Egyptian mysteries in *Osiris and the Egyptian Resurrection* (1911), said: "Both Plutarch and Diodorus agree in assigning a divine origin to Osiris, and both state that he reigned in the form of a man upon the earth. This being so, it is clear that the Egyptians generally believed that a god made himself incarnate, and that an immediate ancestor of the first Pharaoh of Egypt was a being who possessed two natures, the one human and the other divine."[8]

Like the stories of Atlantean gods who had taught primitive humanity the ways of civilization, the tales of Osiris and Isis depict these benevolent gods as the beings responsible for bringing humankind out of savagery and barbarism. Sir James G. Frazer referred to this in his famous work *Adonis, Attis, Osiris: Studies in the History of Oriental Religion*:

> Before his time the Egyptians had been cannibals. But Isis, the sister and wife of Osiris, discovered wheat and barley growing wild, and Osiris introduced the cultivation of these grains amongst his people, who forthwith abandoned cannibalism and took kindly to a corn diet. Moreover, Osiris is said to have been the first to gather fruit from trees, to train the vines to poles, and to tread the grapes. Eager to communicate these beneficent discoveries to all mankind, he committed the whole government of Egypt to his wife Isis, and traveled over the world, diffusing the blessings of civilization wherever he went.[9]

Egyptian scriptures state: "In the beginning was Isis, Oldest of the Old. She was the Goddess from whom all becoming arose."[10] Isis is often depicted suckling her son Horus with her divine essence that kept the gods and all other creatures alive. Like the Mesopotamian version of the great Mother Goddess, her blood was considered holy, and the myths about the couple placed particular emphasis on Osiris's reproductive function. Predictably, the Egyptian royalty, much like the ruling class of Mesopotamia, made every attempt to trace its lineage back to the sacred couple by blood, and even reverted to consanguineous mating to keep the royal line pure. It was Osiris and Isis, the Egyptians claimed, along with their associates and descendants, who taught humanity how to read, write, farm, build, and worship properly. And this story was believed by Pharaoh and slave alike.

The English word "paradise" is derived from the Old Persian word *pairadaese,* which literally means "a walled garden." The Persians believed that they were the descendants of those who escaped an ancient sacred garden after a great flood, and their mythology is rich with the idea of gods who roamed the earth in primordial times. The ancient Avestic scriptures of Persia take us back to a paradisiacal garden on earth, when the ancestors of the Iranian people lived in the fabled *Airyana Vaejo,* the mythical birthplace and original home of the Aryan race. This walled garden had a mild climate, was extremely fertile, and had meadows flowing with rivers, much like Plato's Atlantis.

Like the Greek Poseidon, the Mesopotamian Enki, and the Egyptian Osiris, the Persian god Mithra descended to earth from the heavens with an altruistic mission and eventually became the holy protector of the Persian kings of old, who preserved their bloodline and traced it to divine origins. According to the myths, Mithra's sacrifice insured that the holy blood and divine genes of the gods reached earth, where every creature on earth was shaped with an admixture of the holy seed. It gave to the world all useful herbs, plants, and the all-important wheat. The great early scholar of Mithraism, Franz Cumont, wrote in *The Mysteries of Mithra* (1903) that due to this heroic sacrifice, Mithra "became the creator of all the beneficent beings on earth," and, soon after, "was charged with keeping a watchful eye over his privileged race."[11]

Even in Rome, yet another divine pair, Cybele and Attis, were celebrated and worshipped for their role in giving civilization to humanity. The cult of Cybele was in fact part of the Roman state religion. The goddess Cybele, Goddess of the Mountain, was regarded as the founder of agriculture and law.[12] Her official Roman name was *Mater Deum Magna Idaea,* or Great Idaean Mother of the Gods, and her image was carried in awesome state through the streets of Rome. In *The Woman's Encyclopaedia of Myths and Secrets* (1983), Barbara G. Walker writes: "Roman emperors like Augustus, Claudius, and Antoninus Pius regarded her as the supreme deity of the empire. Augustus established his home facing her temple, and looked upon his wife, the empress Livia Augusta, as an earthly incarnation of her. The Emperor Julian wrote an impassioned address to her."[13] As elsewhere, the sacred rituals devoted to these gods had much to do with the supposed holy bloodline of the Roman Emperors.

Flood of Evidence

...on that day all the fountains of the great deep were broken up, and the windows of heaven were opened.

— Genesis 7:11

Few people today know or care much about these ancient gods and their legends, but quintessential aspects of their story can be found in some very familiar places. As seen earlier, the basic legend described the appearance of powerful gods on earth who proceeded to uplift the mortal races and urge them toward civilization. However, in time these superior peoples mated with the natives on earth and subsequently lost their special genetic character, thus becoming warlike and hungry for power. In the Greek variation, Zeus then sends a great flood, and seals the doom of Atlantis. Remarkably, this scenario is almost identical to God's judgment on erring mankind as described in the Bible (Genesis 6:4-17):

> There were giants on the earth in those days, and also afterward, when the sons of God came in to the daughters of men and they bore children to them. Those were the mighty men who were of old, men of renown. Then the Lord saw that the wickedness of man was great in the earth, and that every intent of the

thoughts of his heart was only evil continually. And the Lord was sorry that He had made man on the earth, and He was grieved in His heart. So the Lord said, "I will destroy man whom I have created from the face of the earth. . . . I myself am bringing floodwaters on the earth, to destroy from under heaven all flesh in which is the breath of life; every thing that is on the earth shall die."

Figure 2:1
Colossal statue of Gilgamesh, who was the world's earliest epical hero, whose tale was found scattered throughout the ancient Mesopotamian world.

The Greek and biblical stories are uncannily similar: Both describe a powerful race that was larger than life in every way—a race of divine origin whose superior genes were mixed with those of regular mortals. The Atlanteans came from the heavens, as did the biblical "giants on the earth." These "mighty men of renown" eventually became so wicked that God, or Zeus—as the case may be—destroyed their home with a great flood.

Scholars have known for decades that the tale of Noah's flood in the Bible was actually a reformulation of the flood story described in the *Gilgamesh Epic.* Imagine the astonishment of scholars a century and a half ago, upon unearthing and deciphering a large body of cuneiform tablets in southern Iraq dating back to 3500 B.C., when they discovered pre-biblical versions of the stories of Adam and Eve, the Tree of Life, the serpent, and the great deluge. Unlike the biblical tale, however, the *Gilgamesh Epic* does not describe a worldwide flood but rather an isolated disaster that occurred in the land of the gods after their fall from grace. This disaster was said to have forced the gods to leave their homes and reestablish their civilization elsewhere.

Various translations of the *Gilgamesh Epic* were subsequently found all over the Middle East and even Israel. For example, a fragment of the Babylonian epic dating from about 1400 B.C. was found at Megiddo in Israel. This proves that the Mesopotamian prototype of the biblical story of the deluge was current in Palestine long before the Hebrews, under Joshua, conquered that land around 1200 B.C. The creation story in Genesis, therefore, is a reworking of older ideas which were based on cosmological compilations gathered through many millennia. In *History Begins at Sumer* (1959), Samuel Kramer writes: "The literature created by the Sumerians left its deep impress on the Hebrews, and one of the thrilling aspects of reconstructing and translating Sumerian belles lettres consists in tracing resemblances and parallels between Sumerian and Biblical literary motifs."[14]

As we have seen, the original legend—the one that pervaded the ancient world—was that gods from other worlds came to an already populated earth, on a mission. The biblical version, which has since shaped the beliefs of all three of the world's most popular religions, was a corrupted form of these earlier myths. As emphasized by Theodore Ziolkowski in *The Sin of Knowledge: Ancient Themes and Modern Variations* (2000): "Clearly, the Hebrew storyteller who wrote the second narrative was drawing on a common pool of ancient Near Eastern folkloric elements, which he combined in a new configuration but with profound psychological insight and with a wholly original emphasis."[15]

We have perhaps no better evidence of a pre-biblical, primeval civilization than that found in the Bible itself (Genesis 4:1–17), namely, the assertion that after killing Abel, Cain went to the land of Nod to get himself a wife. As there were supposedly only three humans on earth at that time—Adam, Eve, and Cain—this is an obvious mistake. Moreover, we are told that Cain received a mark, "lest anyone finding him should kill him," after which he traveled to Nod and built an entire city!

Even in the relatively young Islamic traditions, Adam and Eve were not just exalted human beings but were, rather, "descended from Paradise." God had sent them to earth, and Adam appeared in Ceylon (Sarandib) while Eve descended to Jidda in Arabia, where they had 40,000 children before they died.[16] The destruction of Eden, the flooding of Atlantis, and Noah's deluge may all stem from a common source.

The world's best-known writer on the subject of Plato's Atlantis is Ignatius Donnelly, a nineteenth century congressman from Minnesota who turned to history and mythology in his later years, eventually producing a highly popular and influential book, *Atlantis: The Antediluvian World* in 1882. The book was so successful that it went through 23 printings by 1890 and has remained in print to this day. He began this seminal work by boldly claiming that Atlantis "is not, as has been long supposed, fable, but veritable history." He then proceeded to link the Atlantis story to other legends, claiming that "[Atlantis] was the true Antediluvian world; the Garden of Eden; the Gardens of the Hesperides; the Elysian Fields; the Gardens of Alcinous; the Mesomphalos; the Olympos; the Asgard of the traditions of the ancient nations; representing the universal memory of a great land, where early mankind dwelt for ages in peace and happiness."[17]

In addition, there are lesser-known stories of the flood such as the myth of Deucalion, whom the Greeks believed to be the ancestor of the Hellenic race. In this legend, he and his wife build an ark to escape a flood sent by Zeus and they alone survive after landing on Mount Parnassus. Similarly, in ancient Indian mythology it was the legendary figure Manu, the first king and supposed ancestor of the royal bloodline of India, who was warned by a deity to build an ark to escape the coming flood. He eventually landed on a mountaintop as the sole survivor and performed sacrifices by pouring libations in the waves, which later gave birth to a woman. Reminiscent of the story of Adam and Eve, this couple became the ancestors of the new human race that would go on to replenish the earth.

In general, the great flood was seen by the ancients as the punishment and destruction of a prehistoric world that had, over time, become corrupted and lost its virtue. Such a degenerated world, according to ancient interpreters, was rightly put out of its misery by the hand of divinity, which purified life once more through a great flood that washed away evil and seeded the earth with a new order. The world was "baptized" by the flood, and thus reborn through it. The ritual of expiation by water is still enacted by numerous religions today and, for those who know its origins, it is symbolic of a story as old as time.

The legend of the flooded garden continues to fascinate humanity simply because it is the missing link to our understanding of the sequence of prehistoric events, much as genetic "missing links" in our biological evolution continue to confound modern science. Our ancestors, however, were not perplexed. They believed that our metamorphosis from savagery to civility was directly attributable to intermingling with a superior race of gods. We may reject such notions as superstitions, but not so long ago, great civilizations worldwide revolved around these very beliefs.

Why did each separate culture believe that the blood of these gods was something unique and special, even holy, and that their own people had inherited a portion of it? For what reason would all these nations and races, separated by thousands of miles, uniformly believe that the arts of civilization were *revealed* to humanity by some extraordinary race that lived on a paradisiacal garden somewhere on earth?

Answering these intriguing questions, however, is not our focus here. The aim of this work is to point to the actual island of Atlantis rather than to follow the trail of its story as it affected various cultures. The preceding brief glimpse into world mythology was provided only to show the historic foundation upon which the legend of Atlantis and the related story of the Garden of Eden rests, and to give a sense of its powerful legacy through time. We shall now put aside the supernatural aspects of the Atlantis legend and concentrate on the clues about the location of the island itself.

In the next chapter we shall examine evidence that some great natural catastrophe may have occurred in our early history that submerged an island harboring an advanced civilization. Plato's *Critias* provides the most detailed description of the physical characteristics of Atlantis, and we will focus on this description for the remainder of the book. As we will see in the next chapter, there is far more to the story of Atlantis than its eccentric mythology.

3

Paradise Lost

*There is nothing more visible than what is secret,
and nothing more manifest than what is minute.*

— Confucius
Doctrine of the Mean (600 B.C.)

As I have suggested, Plato's description of Atlantis was not just a prelude to another philosophical dialogue on the ideal society, it was in fact a genuine record of Solon's account of an actual civilization of great antiquity. In this chapter we turn to Plato's actual depiction of Atlantis, examining the almost fifty clues that he provides. These crucial statements from Plato, coupled with our survey of the vast Atlantean literature and world mythology— along with original evidence from empirical data that is offered later in this book—lead us to our hypothesis of the location of the legendary island.

This chapter also provides a close look at Plato's descriptions of the physical aspects of Atlantis as well as features of the capital and cultural center of the island—Atlantis City itself. I will compile a list of clues over the course of the chapter that will consist of direct statements by Plato or inferences that can be reasonably derived from the text of the *Critias* or *Timaeus*.

The Island and the Flood

One of the most salient features of Plato's account is his claim that Atlantis was submerged under water around 9600 B.C. by a combination of catastrophic events—a tremendous earthquake accompanied by a calamitous flood. If this description is factual, then the first physical fact we can infer is that the island was located in an area close to active tectonic plates, and it was vulnerable to considerable seismic and volcanic activity.

As to the general appearance of the landmass, Plato gives us the primary clue in this passage from the *Critias*:

> To begin with the region as a whole was said to be high above the level of the sea, from which it rose precipitously.[1]

From the perspective of an approaching ship at sea, Atlantis must have presented a rather striking profile. Sailors would have seen a landmass rising abruptly from the ocean that was capped with mountains, which, as he points out, were jutting "high above" the sea level.

But if Atlantis rose to such a height, then we are faced with questions about the kind of flood that could have swallowed this rather formidable piece of land.

If we are to take Plato's story literally, this was obviously no ordinary flood. If indeed the "region as a whole" (i.e., the whole island) was highly elevated, then even a great flood would have merely affected the lower elevations and could not have risen hundreds or even thousands of feet above the original sea level.[2] An earthquake-generated tsunami—being no more than an abrupt but temporary elevation of water—could not explain the disappearance of Atlantis either. A more reasonable hypothesis is that Atlantis was already located in a basin of sorts that was subsequently *filled in* by a tremendous body of water—a flood great enough to bring in the volume of water necessary to reach such a great height.

However, we must bear in mind that not everything was submerged. Plato clearly indicates in the *Timaeus* that some portion of the island remained near the surface of the water, explaining it as the reason "why the sea in that area is to this day impassible to navigation, which is hindered by mud just below the surface, the remains of the sunken island."[3] This statement offers another clue—one that has led many researchers to speculate that the highest elevations of Atlantis may still be visible. Some have pointed out that those higher places would have provided a refuge for Atlanteans escaping the flood and would therefore still be visible today. In *The Atlantis Myth* (1948), H.S. Bellamy summarizes this part of the legend: "The lowland dwellers who survived the cataclysm took refuge among the inhabitants of the highlands. . . . *The Atlantis myth* contains only indirect references, but in Greek traditional lore we find some significant passages. . . . these survivors repeopled 'the world'."[4]

So let us quickly retrace our steps in this section. So far we have inferred that Plato's Atlantis was an island that rose precipitously from the sea to a considerable height. A catastrophic flood submerged the whole island, possibly leaving its mountaintops above water. Atlantis may have been located in a basin or depression during an era of lower sea levels that was subsequently filled in by a tremendous body of water. Also, small islands near Atlantis served as stepping-stones to other continents.[5] And these items cover all Plato said regarding the physical structure of the island or "region" as a whole.

In the following section we will continue to build our catalog of facts and inferences based on Plato's account. We turn now to his remarkable description of the great plain of Atlantis and the residential center of Atlantis City.

Atlantis Proper

*It may be, as some indeed suspect, that the science we
see as the dawn of recorded history was not science at its
dawn, but represents the remnants of the science of some
great and as yet untraced civilization.*

— S.R.K. Glanville
The Legacy of Egypt (1942)

Earlier we learned that according to the Egyptian priests, the gods
amiably divided the territories of earth amongst themselves,
allotting the island of Atlantis to Poseidon. As the story goes,
Poseidon's offspring began to create a high civilization on the
island, dividing it into ten parts. His eldest son, Atlas, was given his
mother's home district (Atlantis City) and the land surrounding it,
while the younger offspring were made governors of various
districts across the land. The name "Atlantis" was in fact taken
from Poseidon's first-born son, Atlas.

We are also told that, in time, these dignified and gentle
people extended their civilizing mission to the indigenous peoples
near and far.

Atlantis proper—the main residential district—was said to be
a large flat area on an otherwise mountainous island. The major
cities of Atlantis Island were located on this long and rectangular
plain that lay at the foothills. This elongated plain, in turn,
surrounded the capital of the island, which Plato calls "Atlantis
City." Here is the geographic detail:

> At the centre of the island (i.e., midway along its great-
> est length), near the sea, was a plain, said to be the
> most beautiful and fertile of all plains, and near the
> middle of this plain about fifty stades inland a hill of no
> great size.[6]

Apparently, Atlantis City was situated near the middle of the
longest length of a rectangular coastal plain. And, it was built

around an elevation "of no great size" that Plato later refers to as "Acropolis Hill." And we are told that this hill was located about fifty stades (about six miles) from the sea.[7] Plato continues:

> The city [i.e., Atlantis City] was surrounded by a uniformly flat plain, which was in turn enclosed by mountains which came right down to the sea. This plain was rectangular in shape, measuring three thousand stades in length and at its midpoint two thousand stades in breadth from the coast. This whole area of the island faced south, and was sheltered from the north winds. The mountains which surrounded it were celebrated as being more numerous, higher, and more beautiful than any which exist today.[8]

With just a few citations from the *Critias,* it is possible to gather a number of helpful clues with which to construct a hypothetical model of Atlantis. Here then is a list of statements that we have so far derived from Plato's text:

1. Atlantis Island rose sharply from the sea.
2. There were smaller islands nearby that served as stepping-stones to opposite continents.
3. The mountainous island rose to a high level above the sea.
4. The cities of Atlantis were situated on a plain.
5. The capital of Atlantis Island was Atlantis City, which was near the middle of a fertile plain.
6. The plain was long and rectangular.
7. Mountains that came right down to the sea enclosed the plain.
8. The plain was uniformly flat.
9. The plain was beautiful, fertile, and near the sea.
10. The capital of Atlantis was situated roughly six miles from the sea.
11. The plain of Atlantis faced south.
12. The plain was 3,000 stades (340 miles) long and 2,000 stades (227 miles) wide.

13. The cities on the plain were sheltered from the cold northerly winds.[9]

14. The mountains that surrounded Atlantis were "numerous, higher, and more beautiful than any which exist today."

A bit more extrapolation can provide still more useful statements. For instance, if most of the mountainous island was submerged by the great flood, then the plain that was lying in the lowest elevations must now rest in deep waters as part of the seafloor. Also, if the plain was long and rectangular and "faced south," then it must have stretched in an east/west direction. Furthermore, the rectangular plain is said to lay midway along the *greatest length* of the island, which would seem to indicate that the island itself must have also stretched in an east/west direction. We can likewise deduce that since the Plain of Atlantis was sheltered from the cold *northerly* winds, then the island must have been in the Northern Hemisphere; otherwise, any cold winds would have been coming from the south. We can now add these three new propositions to the list:

15. Both the island and its southern plain were elongated.

16. They ran parallel with one another in an east/west direction.

17. The island was north of the equator.

The famous map at Figure 3:1 is a relatively good portrayal of Plato's description of Atlantis as we have encountered it so far. On October 20, 1912, the *New York American* published this celebrated map with an accompanying article by a man named Paul Schliemann. The author claimed he was the grandson of Heinrich Schliemann—the discoverer of Troy—and further claimed to have found the map in his grandfather's papers. Paul's true identity has never been confirmed, and the Atlantean artifacts that he claimed to possess never surfaced, but the map is nonetheless a useful tool for our purposes. It can in fact serve as an indication of the kind of formation one might expect to observe on the seafloor.[10] Note that the mountain peaks of Atlantis reach high into the air, helping us to envision the magnitude of flooding that would have been required to cover most of the island.

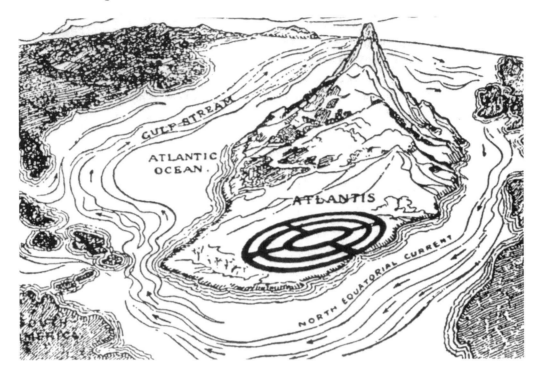

Figure 3:1
Early depiction of Atlantis. This famous map of
Atlantis was a milestone in speculative Atlantology.

Plato also indicates that to provide for fresh water, the Atlanteans dug a large rectangular channel around the whole Plain of Atlantis in order to collect the rainwater that ran down from the highlands. Here's how he states it:

> It was naturally a long, regular rectangle; and any defects in its shape were corrected by means of a ditch dug round it. . . . The rivers which flowed down from the mountains emptied into it, and it made a complete circuit of the plain, running round to the city from both directions, and there discharging into the sea.[11]

According to another part of Plato's account, the weather system of Atlantis was governed by highland precipitation; the leeward plains and lowlands were relatively arid. We can infer that the summers must have been hot and dry, which in turn would have necessitated the building of an extensive canal system, just as Plato indicated. This "ditch dug round" the rectangular plain would be needed to capture and preserve the fresh water from the highlands.

Considerable amounts of water must have been required to irrigate a large plain during the growing season on Atlantis. If we can assume that what Plato calls "cold northerly winds" brought snow to the higher elevations, we can infer that periodic melting of snow would have been a prime source of runoff water that was routed into the irrigation system, water that was not available through precipitation on the lowlands. Obviously, cycles of this nature are indicative of seasonal variations on the island. In looking at this scenario, we can further conclude that Atlantis must have been located neither too close to, nor too far from the equator, for there to be such moderate weather variation and gradation. We have already located Atlantis in the northern latitudes, and we can now infer that the island had to be some-where between a tropical zone and a colder northern temperate zone.

Our list has now grown to include these new items:

18. Atlantis had both a winter and a summer.

19. Atlantis was neither very close nor very far from the equator.

20. The plain was in a valley.

21. There was snowfall on the high mountain peaks of Atlantis.

22. The island's rivers originated on the highlands.

Atlantis City

At the same time, and an age after or more, the inhabitants
of the great Atlantis did flourish. . . . the magnificent temple, palace,
city, and hill; and the manifold streams of goodly navigable rivers,
which as so many chains environed the same site and temple; and
the several degrees of ascent, where by men did climb up to the
same, as if it had been a Scala Coeli. . . .

— Sir Francis Bacon
The New Atlantis (1626)

Although Plato wrote little concerning the cities on the island of
Atlantis, he gave detailed descriptions and dimensions of Atlantis
City itself. We have already learned that it was located on the
slopes of "a hill of no great size", and that it was known as
Acropolis Hill.[12] This hill was also called Mt. Atlas and was named
after Atlas, first son of Poseidon, in his role as Pillar of the Sky.

The sacred hill was described by Plato and in other legends
as a sophisticated and advanced home for the gods, their children,
and a corps of trusted mortals at their service. It was from the
summit of this cosmic mountain that knowledge and wisdom
were bestowed for the benefit of humanity. In these precincts
dwelled the great goddess, well cared for and protected, living in
luxury, and isolated from the brutal world outside the island. The
Atlantean race were her progeny. They supposedly originated
within the confines of a circular, golden wall that surrounded the
lush garden at the summit of the Acropolis Hill, which was the
holiest spot on the entire island.[13]

The Acropolis was protected in an ingenious way. Three huge
circular canals were dug around this hill, extending outwards from
the base and interspersed by enclosed rings of land. Viewed
from afar, the water-filled canals would have formed three large
blue concentric circles around the summit of the hill. Being
surrounded by rings of canals, the Acropolis would have resembled

a small island of sorts, appearing like a bulls-eye in the middle of the concentric canals.

This barrier of land and water made the holy mountain completely inaccessible to the uninvited. One could only enter the sacred home of the gods by permission and then by passing through the massive, encircling walls and the connecting bridges. Plato wrote:

> [Poseidon] fortified the hill...by enclosing it with concentric rings of sea and land. There were two rings of land and three of sea, like cartwheels, with the island at their centre and equidistant from each other, making the place inaccessible to man (for there were still no ships or sailing in those days). He equipped the central island with godlike lavishness. . . .[14]

Plato's description of the Acropolis Hill, much like his portrayal of the rectangular plain, is laden with specific measurements. This meticulous account in particular reveals the detailed nature of Plato's understanding of the Atlantis story. For example, he reports the presence of a canal "fifty stades long" (5.7 miles) by one half of a stade (300 feet) wide. This huge canal ran from a point on the outermost of the three concentric canals all the way to the southern coast, thus making the city accessible by water from the sea. They also built bridges over the canal and tunnels under it in their effort to guard Acropolis Hill.

According to Plato, the Acropolis Hill itself had a diameter measuring about twenty-seven stades, or three miles. The hill and the outer city districts were enclosed by "a circular stone wall" with a diameter of fourteen miles. This massive wall extended to the southern coast, where the canal emptied into the sea. The diameter and width of each canal, the rings of land they encircled, the layout of the central hill area, and the outer wall are each described with sufficient precision to permit an accurate scaling and modeling of Atlantis City.

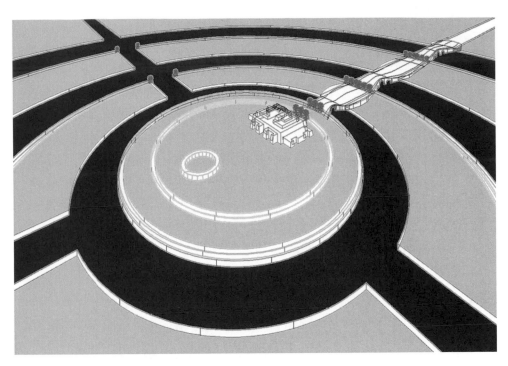

Figure 3:2
Layout of the Acropolis Hill area according to an artist's conception.
Based on Plato's description in the *Critias*. (Art by Bo Atkinson)

Figure 3:3
Artist's conception of the Acropolis Hill. (Art by Bo Atkinson)

From the discussion above let us add a few more propositions to our growing list:

23. The Acropolis Hill was about 3 miles in diameter.

24. The Acropolis Hill was a low mountain.

25. The outer stone wall that surrounded Atlantis City was circular and had a diameter of about 14 miles.

26. The outer stone wall met the southern sea area and was about seven miles away from the base of the Acropolis Hill.

From the measurements provided by Plato we can see that his numbers—at least when it comes to recreating a city plan—are consistent and workable. Given the report that the Atlantean ships entered the city along the southern coast, we can infer that:

27. The Plain of Atlantis must have been at or near sea level.

The latter point is corroborated by Plato's statement that the plain was surrounded by mountains which "descended right down to the sea." In other words, the coastal hills at the southern edge of the plain separated it from the sea, but the plain itself must have been at or around sea level. There is additional confirmation of this from the Greek myth of the Garden of the Hesperides, yet another name for Atlantis. According to the legend, "the outer edge of the garden was slightly raised, so that the water might not run in and overflow the land."[15]

Plato seems to have spared no effort to describe the city as accurately as possible. After all, this was supposedly the actual residence of the gods who ruled Atlantis and taught humanity the arts of civilization. If we are to take Plato's account of Atlantis literally, then Acropolis Hill was the source of civilizing education for all of the natives encountered by the Atlanteans. As we shall see in upcoming chapters, the symbolic layout of Atlantis City, regardless of its factual basis, became the template for many of the structural designs that have been passed down to us as "classical architecture."

Atlantis City
Northern Mountains

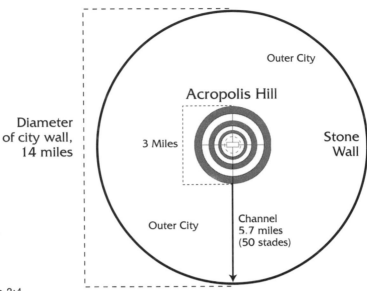

Outer City

Acropolis Hill

Diameter
of city wall,
14 miles

3 Miles

Stone
Wall

Outer City

Channel
5.7 miles
(50 stades)

Figure 3:4
City plan of the capital.
(scaled to size)

Acropolis Hill

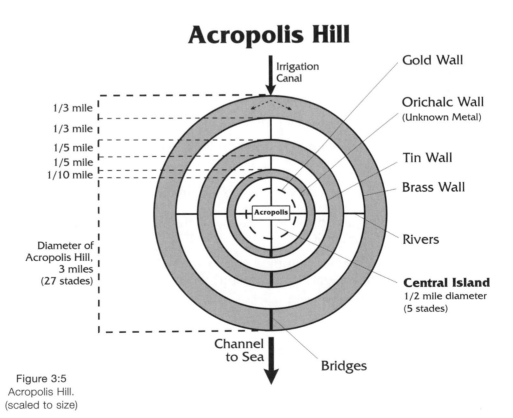

Irrigation
Canal

Gold Wall

Orichalc Wall
(Unknown Metal)

1/3 mile

1/3 mile

1/5 mile

1/5 mile

1/10 mile

Tin Wall

Brass Wall

Acropolis

Rivers

Diameter of
Acropolis Hill,
3 miles
(27 stades)

Central Island
1/2 mile diameter
(5 stades)

Channel
to Sea

Bridges

Figure 3:5
Acropolis Hill.
(scaled to size)

More Facts about the Island

These are the immortal goddesses who lay with mortal men and bore them children like unto gods.

— Hesiod
Theogony (700 B.C.)

According to legend, Atlantis was initially a land of great beauty, ingenious engineering and architecture, abundant food supply, and glorious peace. Here, the so-called gods, goddesses, cherubs, and seraphim played among the lush greenery as they gently taught the native human race how to live a civilized and peaceful life. It was the epitome of how humanity imagines life in the Golden Age.

In our quest to find Atlantis we are provided with more than physical details about the shape of the island and the city; there are other clues as well. For example, in the *Critias* (114c-e), the wealth of the Atlanteans is described along with the extent of their dominion over the Mediterranean coastal territories. Plato also describes (114e-115b) the island's self-sufficiency and its considerable natural resources, including precious metals, timber, wild and domesticated animals (including elephants), aromatic substances, roots, herbs, bushes, gums, flowers, fruits, cultivated crops, cereals, and pulse. Says Plato, "all these were produced by that sacred island, then still beneath the sun, in wonderful quality and profusion."

We have these clues to add to an already long list:

28. The island provided almost all the requirements for human life.

29. The Atlanteans mined solid materials as well as various metals on the island.

30. Atlantis had gold.

31. Atlantis had silver.

32. Atlantis had copper.

33. Atlantis had tin.

34. Atlantis had precious stones.

35. Timber was plentiful.

36. Atlantis had black, yellow, and white rocks that were used for construction.

37. The island had marshes, swamps, rivers, mountains, and a plain.

38. Atlantis had roots, herbs, bushes, gums, fruits, and flowers.

39. There were crops, cereals, pulse, and oils in "wonderful quality and profusion."

40. There were elephants on the island.

Other interesting facts also stand out in Plato's account. It seems that Poseidon had caused two springs to flow on the island:

> He made two springs flow, one of hot and one of cold water, and caused the earth to grow abundant produce of every kind.[16]

The presence of a hot spring means that the island was composed at least in part of igneous rock (hardened lava). This point is often taken by researchers to mean that Atlantis was a volcanic mountain and that the destruction of the island was due to a massive volcanic eruption, even though there is no direct mention made of volcanoes in the *Critias*. But the allusion to a hot spring provides more clues:

41. The island contained igneous rock.

42. Atlantis had a hot spring and a cold spring.

43. Atlantis was located on or around an area that experienced volcanic activity.

Taken as a whole, this large set of physical clues has significant implications in the search for Atlantis: the accumulated detail has now become sufficient to narrow the search to specific regions on the planet. Let us review the main findings: We have a rough geographical description of the island as a whole; the location of the plain, relative to the whole landmass; and the location of the low mountain that served as the heart of the island's capital. In addition, we have clues regarding the kinds of animals on the island, its weather patterns, metals, and to some extent, its flora and fauna. All that remains now is to narrow the search further by estimating its size and location.

The Location and Size of the Island

See simplicity in the complicated.

— Lao Tsu
Tao Te Ching (600 B.C.)

Of all the clues provided by Plato about Atlantis, none has created more controversy and confusion than those pertaining to its location. These clues are so vague that his words are routinely interpreted to fit practically any place on earth, from South America to Malaysia to the Antarctic.

Figure 3:6
The known world according to Hecataeus (500 B.C.), as envisioned one hundred years after Solon's trip to Egypt.

But let us first contextualize the problem. Today we are all familiar with the shape and location of the world's major landmasses, but this was hardly so in Plato's time; his generation knew very little of geography. It would be another 2,000 years before there was even general agreement that the world was round (although, to their credit, some early Greek and Egyptian scientists envisioned the likelihood that the earth was a sphere).

It is in the *Timaeus* that we find the only location clues for Atlantis, as described by the Egyptian priests:

> Our records tell how your city checked a great power which arrogantly advanced from its base in the Atlantic Ocean to attack the cities of Europe and Asia. For in those days the Atlantic was navigable. There was an island opposite the strait which you call (so you say) the Pillars of Heracles, an island larger than Libya and Asia combined; from it travellers could in those days reach the other islands, and from the whole opposite continent which surrounds what can truly be called the ocean.[17]

This statement would appear to locate Atlantis in what we today call the Atlantic Ocean; but the problems with this interpretation are manifold. The greatest difficulty is our incomplete knowledge of what the ancients meant by the "Pillars of Heracles" (or Hercules). Some researchers assume that the Egyptians were referring to the Strait of Gibraltar. But in *The Flood from Heaven: Deciphering the Atlantis Legend* (1992), Eberhard Zangger explains that according to the poet Servius (400 A.D.), the ancients knew of several different Pillars of Hercules. One was located at the Strait of Gibraltar, and others led from the Aegean Sea or into the Black Sea. Because the Strait of Gibraltar had been reached by Greek sailors only shortly before the time of Solon's travel to Egypt, Zangger points to Solon himself as the possible source for all the confusion. He writes: "Thus, when Solon heard about the narrow waterway in a distant place, he naturally thought of the passage into the Atlantic. By using a contemporary perspective he committed the same mistake that would characterize the study of the Atlantis account for the next two and a half millennia. . . . Perhaps Solon helped the priest's translation by providing what he thought were the correct place-names."[18] In other words, it is quite possible that the Pillars of Hercules referred to by the Egyptians in a story said to be 9,000 years old, could have been located in the Aegean Sea, or perhaps other places in the Mediterranean aside from Gibraltar.

To assume without hesitation that the Strait of Gibraltar *must* be the same as the Pillars of Hercules is totally unwarranted. It actually seems absurd to suggest that people living in the eastern Mediterranean region in 9000 B.C. knew about the Strait of Gibraltar, and that they might even use it as *a common point of reference!*

Another discrepancy that has caused the location of Atlantis to be so widely positioned throughout the globe is the confusion about its size. Modern translations of the *Timaeus* state that Atlantis was larger than Libya and Asia combined. But this statement is almost meaningless in a modern context. First of all, the ancients had no accurate information regarding the real size of Asia or of whatever stood for Libya in those days. And second, if Atlantis were somehow the size of a large continent like Asia, and not an island—as interpreted by some—then Plato's scenario of the sudden submergence of such a sizable landmass is almost non-sensical. Another explanation is in order.

One must consider another factor: There may be a discrepancy in Plato's report of the dimensions of the rectangular plain, which he says was the equivalent of 227 miles wide. This contradicts his statement that the city of Atlantis was "near the middle of the plain," only six miles from the coast. If we assume the denotation of "middle of the plain" is the same as "center of the mass," and not "midway between the western and eastern boundaries," (irrespective of latitude) then it becomes difficult to resolve the question of scale, and ultimately the dimensions of Atlantis as a whole. Plato's other stated measurements of the Acropolis Hill and its surroundings are consistent and make it hard to believe he would have made such a glaring mistake. In *The Dimension of Paradise: the Proportions and Symbolic Numbers of Ancient Cosmology* (1988), John Mitchell wrote: "At first the problem of the plain looks simple, even banal; but investigation proves it extremely complicated, capable of many near solutions, none of which is ever quite adequate."[19]

We cannot rely solely on Plato's *Critias* and *Timaeus* to find the actual location or determine the size of Atlantis. There are inconsistencies in the text itself and uncertainties concerning our knowledge of the ancient Egyptian and Greek understanding of regional geography. It is not surprising then that today's camps in Atlantology are divided on the issue of location. Nevertheless, we have before us an unambiguous set of clues concerning many other important features of Atlantis, all of which will be explored in the following chapters. These clues, coupled with new empirical data, will, I believe, offer compelling reasons for our claim to have discovered the location of the sunken isle.

Let us conclude this examination of Plato's text for useful clues. Displayed below is the complete list of propositions we now believe can reasonably be inferred from Plato's account of Atlantis.

1. Atlantis Island rose sharply from the sea.
2. There were smaller islands nearby that served as stepping-stones to an opposite continent.
3. The mountainous island rose to a very high level above the sea.
4. The cities of Atlantis were situated on a plain.
5. The capital of Atlantis Island was Atlantis City, situated near the middle of the plain.
6. The plain was long and rectangular.
7. Mountains that came right down to the sea enclosed the plain, and therefore the city.
8. The plain was uniformly flat.
9. The plain was very beautiful, fertile and near the sea.
10. The capital of Atlantis was situated roughly six miles from the sea.

11. The Plain of Atlantis faced south.

12. The plain was reported to be 3,000 stades (340 miles) long and 2,000 stades (227 miles) wide, but was probably much smaller than that.

13. The cities on the plain were sheltered from the cold northerly winds.

14. The mountains that surrounded Atlantis were "numerous, higher and more beautiful than any which exist today."

15. Both the island and its southern plain were elongated.

16. The island and the plain ran parallel with one another in an east/west direction.

17. The island was north of the equator.

18. Atlantis had both a winter and a summer.

19. Atlantis was neither very close nor very far from the equator.

20. The plain was in a valley.

21. There was snowfall on the high mountain peaks of Atlantis.

22. The island's rivers originated in the highlands.

23. The Acropolis Hill was about three miles in diameter.

24. The Acropolis Hill was a low mountain.

25. The outer stone wall that surrounded Atlantis City was circular and had a diameter of about fourteen miles.

26. The outer stone wall met the southern sea area and was about six miles away from the base of the Acropolis Hill.

27. The plain of Atlantis must have been close to sea level.

28. The island provided almost all the requirements for human life.

29. The Atlanteans mined solid materials as well as various metals on the island.

30. Atlantis had gold.

31. Atlantis had silver.

32. Atlantis had copper.

33. Atlantis had tin.

34. Atlantis had precious stones.

35. Timber was plentiful.

36. Atlantis had black, yellow, and white rocks that were used for construction.

37. The island had marshes, swamps, rivers, mountains, and a plain.

38. Atlantis had roots, herbs, bushes, gums, fruits, and flowers.

39. There were crops, cereals, pulse, and oils in "wonderful quality and profusion."

40. There were elephants on the island.

41. The island was composed of igneous rock.

42. Atlantis had hot springs and cold springs.

43. Atlantis was located on or around an area that experienced volcanic activity.

Plato provided a few other clues which will be discussed in upcoming chapters, including:

44. Atlantis was "swallowed up by the earth."

45. Atlantis was prone to violent seismic activity and flooding.

46. The Atlantean empire embraced three continents: Europe, Asia, and Africa.

47. The island was flooded about 9,600 B.C.

48. Some of the island's highest peaks may still be above water.

4

As Above, So Below

No state can find happiness unless the
artist drawing it uses a divine pattern.

— Plato
Laws (360 B.C.)

In this chapter we will trace the appearance of Atlantean "sacred geometry" and other core images as they were represented by later generations and observe how these forms have been expressed in city squares, temples, monuments, and objects of art. I will offer the suggestion that these designs first appeared on a very large and sophisticated scale on Atlantis and have served ever since as the hazy and distant source of structural motifs that can be found all over the world from ancient Mediterranean and Asian societies to the present-day United States. We hope to illustrate the possibility that across time and cultures, the sacred designs of the Acropolis Hill and its walled city have been recapitulated, albeit unconsciously and unintentionally, in religious and public structures all over the world.

While it is not in the scope of this book to thoroughly detail these influences, a few remarkable details cannot be ignored. We will examine these parallels in this chapter with one primary purpose in mind: to prepare us for the visualization process that is needed to successfully identify, in later chapters, the remains of Atlantis on the eastern Mediterranean seafloor. By studying these later designs we will be better able to recognize their prototypes that, as we suggest in this study, presently lie under the waters off the coast of Cyprus.

In ancient times, art, architecture, urban design, and religion were always tightly linked in the minds of designers. But with Atlantis, this practice went a step further: The geometrical city plan of Atlantis, according to the *Critias,* was said to be *personally designed by the gods themselves;* its majestic proportions reflected the harmonic proportions originally projected by the creator gods into the cosmos itself. In later times, new city plans and sacred art and architecture were copied from these "magical" designs and were believed to invoke the protection of the gods.

Worth noting in particular, as an iconic concept of classical design, is the image presented by the concentric circular canals surrounding the Acropolis Hill, with its radial, spoke-like rivers dividing the circle into quadrants. Plato's description of these circular canals, which he refers to as "cartwheels," indicates that they were fed by four rivers that originated at the summit of the Acropolis and flowed downhill along the cardinal directions. The Acropolis was thus divided into natural quadrants, forming a figure known variously as the "Celtic Circle," the "Maltese Cross," the "Crossed Circle," and, of course, the "Cross of Atlantis." Here is how Ignatius Donnelly put it: "In the great ditch surrounding the whole land like a circle, and into which streams flowed down from the mountains, we probably see the original of the four rivers of Paradise, and the emblem of the cross surrounded by a circle, which, as we will show hereafter, was, from the earliest pre-Christian ages, accepted as the emblem of the Garden of Eden."[1] He continued: "All this cannot be mere coincidence; it points to a common tradition of a veritable land, where four rivers flowed down in opposite directions from a central mountain-peak. And these four rivers, flowing to the north, south, east, and west, constitute the origin of that sign of the Cross which we have seen meeting us at every point among the races who were either descended from the people of Atlantis, or who, by commerce and colonization, received their opinions and civilization from them."[2]

Even a cursory look at the art and architecture of later cultures reveals allusions to the crossed-circle image. For example, the garden style of the old Persian kings, called the *Chahar Bagh* (Four Gardens), was constructed around a central "pool of life" from which four channels of water departed in the form of a cross. And this same pattern can still be seen in the design of the pools at the Taj Mahal.

This sacred symbol must also have made a permanent impression on the ancient races of India and Tibet as can be seen in their ritualistic use of mandalas, sacred circular figures that are sometimes referred to as the "world wheel."

The well-known Tibetan sand mandalas, for example, often appear as a series of concentric circles that surround a square in the "holy center." The square represents the palace or temple that houses the central deity and is used to ritually invoke the divine presence.

Tibetan lamas still employ these mandalas for the purpose of meditation and rites of purification in the belief that the mandala "reflects the world of gods." For example, the construction of a sand mandala begins only after the proper blessing of the materials because the gods "need a clean and pure place to stay."[3] The four-walled palace/temple is encrusted with jewels and faces east, with its elaborate gates marking the cardinal points of the compass. At the highest level of the palace is an eight-petaled lotus where the deity Kalachakra embraces his consort Vishvamata, the All-Mother, together symbolizing the "union of wisdom and compassion."

At the end of the ritual the presiding lama prays and thanks the deities for their participation in the ceremony, asking them to leave the mandala and return to their heavenly homes. The sand is then brushed toward the center of the platform, placed in urns, and transported to a nearby body of water. While the praying and chanting proceeds, the sand is ritualistically emptied into the water, thus injecting the perfect peace of the gods into the everyday world.[4] Might this elaborate ritual evoke an ancient connection between visiting gods, Tibetan mandalic symbols, and the original Atlantean designs?

To this day, Hindu temples are also built around a mandala design. Known as *vastupurusamandala,* this design concept is comprised of a square surrounded by circles. As a matter of tradition, this mandala is etched on the earth before the temple is built, and the square is oriented to the four cardinal points of the compass.

Could it be that these Persian, Tibetan, and Hindu designs are an echo of a memory whose source is long forgotten, but in reality stems from Atlantean sacred symbols? The similarities seem to point to those far-distant times on the legendary isle whose capital city was laid out in a vast mandala and whose central precincts were the residences of godlike beings.

Stairway to Heaven

A nation of navigators, then. And a nation of builders, too: Tiahuanaco builders, Teotihuacan builders, pyramid builders, Sphinx builders, builders who could lift and position 200-ton blocks of limestone with apparent ease, builders who could align vast monuments to the cardinal points with uncanny accuracy. Whoever they were, these builders appeared to have left their characteristic fingerprints all over the world in the form of cyclopean polygonal masonry, site layouts involving astronomical alignments, mathematical and geodetic puzzles, and myths about gods in human form.

— Graham Hancock
Fingerprints of the Gods (1995)

We can also imagine the echo of Atlantis's sacred forms and symbols in "classic" architecture. Spherical domes are found atop Orthodox and Catholic Christian churches, Islamic mosques, and Buddhist stupas. The Temple Mount in Jerusalem is a walled, rectangular fortress built on the summit of a mountain; at its center stands the circular Dome of the Rock, a huge mosque that is covered in gold. The city of Mecca in Saudi Arabia is also a walled, rectangular fortress, where worshippers pray as they circumambulate Islam's holiest site.

The Acropolis Hill of Atlantis is depicted as a step pyramid that led up to the abode of the gods. If the culture of Atlantis was as influential as this and other studies suggest, then the cultural legacy of this form may indeed have served as the archetype for ziggurats, pyramids, and other sacred structures around the world. From South America and Mexico to Mesopotamia, Greece, Rome, Persia, India, Egypt, and the Far East, researchers have verified that such structures were believed to connect mankind with the gods, who supposedly lived high atop the holy mountain. Henri Frankfort commented on this phenomenon in his book *Birth of Civilization in the Near East* (1959): "From the 'mountain' he (the god) comes forth at the New Year when nature revives. Thus the 'mountain' is essentially the mysterious sphere of activity of the superhuman powers. The Sumerians created the conditions under which communication with the gods became possible when they erected the artificial mountains for their temples."[5]

It hardly seems a coincidence that the figure of the sacred mountain pervades much of world culture. In Mesopotamian mythology, the Tree of Immortal Life is often depicted as growing on a sacred mountain. The Hanging Gardens in Babylon, one of the ancient world's Seven Wonders, were shaped like a terraced, artificial mountain rising off the plain. Covered with beautiful trees and flowers, it was watered by a source that began at the peak of the pyramidal structure. In India the Acropolis Hill may have

Figure 4:1
This pyramid at Dahshour, Egypt, may echo the original step-pyramid that according to Plato led up to the abode of the gods on Acropolis Hill at Atlantis. Similar designs can be seen in ziggurats, pyramids, and other sacred structures that appeared in later millennia around the world.

been remembered as Mt. Meru, a golden mountain that served as the "axis of the world." It was the home of the wise and powerful gods who kept the world from falling into chaos.

The Greek version of an acropolis (originally a Greek word meaning "city at the top") was a "low mountain of no great size" that was the center of social and religious life of a city. Its establishment as a local home for the gods was a basic requirement in the founding of Greek city-states. The Acropolis at Athens, often called the "sacred rock," was a centrally located elevation that supported and protected the most sacred of temples. We saw earlier how the goddess was always resident in the temple atop Acropolis Hill in Atlantis. Similarly, the Parthenon at Athens once contained a gigantic statue made of gold and ivory that depicted the patron goddess of the city, Athena, the Goddess of Knowledge. She later appeared as the Roman goddess Minerva.

Plato was born only ten years after the completion of the temples atop the Athenian Acropolis. He must have marveled at

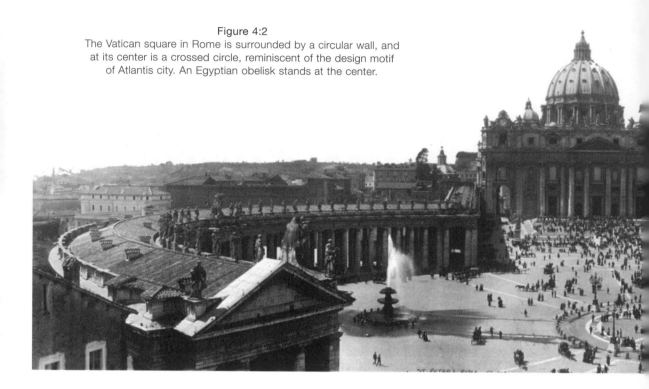

Figure 4:2
The Vatican square in Rome is surrounded by a circular wall, and at its center is a crossed circle, reminiscent of the design motif of Atlantis city. An Egyptian obelisk stands at the center.

this symbol of the ancient goddess that so vividly harks back to the majestic days of Atlantis that he enshrined in the *Critias*. He might have even used the gymnasiums that were placed at the base of the Acropolis, much like those that he said were located on the original Acropolis Hill on Atlantis. Although it has long been considered a mystery, the magnificent Parthenon Frieze, sculpted around the top of the giant structure, could well be depicting key images from Plato's Atlantis, including the council of the gods and their legendary contributions to human civilization.[6]

We know that after he finished writing the *Critias,* Plato began to produce what would become one of his best-known works, *Laws*. It could not have been coincidental that the subject of *Laws* was Magnesia, a utopian city-state he wanted to actually build in a depopulated area of Crete. Always the idealistic philosopher, Plato nonetheless sought out practical ways to benefit human society, and this may perhaps explain why he rushed to

write *Laws* in his final years. Having already mastered the "divine pattern" of Atlantis, he may have wished to evoke its legacy for practical use in his own time.

Even Rome bears the fingerprints of the Atlantean iconography. An ancient Egyptian obelisk still stands at the very center of a crossed circle in St. Peter's Square, facing every Pope who addresses a crowd. The square has two fountains and is surrounded by a circular wall.

The Nazi movement was also greatly influenced by the legend of the sunken isle and its godlike citizens. The Nazis were deeply affected by the occult, and, to them, Atlantis was no myth. When the young Hitler joined the so-called Thule Society it was already comprised of wealthy and influential Germans who believed that they were the direct descendants of the Aryan race, which supposedly held the surviving bloodline of the gods. Thule was a mythical land that is closely associated with the legend of Atlantis.

Hitler's vision of the Third Reich included the belief that some of the godlike priests of Atlantis survived the catastrophic flood and reached the mainland, later giving rise to the Indo-European civilization and the Aryan race. The head of the ruthless Waffen SS, Heinrich Himmler, believed that the Germans were related to the Atlanteans by bloodline.[7] Tall, blonde, and blue-eyed SS troopers were recruited in an effort to create a pure race reminiscent of the Atlanteans. They were sent to impregnate women who supposedly expressed strong Aryan traits, in order to re-create a race of superhumans.

Not surprisingly, the symbol for the Nazi movement, chosen by Hitler himself, was based on "the impression that it was a 'pure Aryan' sign."[8] Prior to its symbolic association with the events of World War II, the swastika represented happiness, fortune and good luck, just as Plato described the island of Atlantis as the most "blessed," "happy," or "fortunate" land. The symbol was prevalent in ancient India, Persia, China, Japan, and even among the Indian tribes of North, Central, and South America.

Could the swastika be related to Atlantean design motifs? Many researchers believe this to be the case. In 1894, Thomas Wilson, the curator of the Department of Prehistoric Anthropology at the U.S. National Museum, presented a comprehensive report on the origin of the swastika symbol entitled, *The Swastika, the earliest known symbol, and its migrations.* He wrote: "Of the many forms of the cross, the Swastika is the most ancient. Despite the theories and speculations of students, its origin is unknown. It began before history, and is properly classed as prehistoric. . . . It is believed by some to have been the *oldest Aryan symbol*."[9] The swastika sign, therefore, may be yet another offshoot of the crossed-circle sign of Atlantis. But its current stigmatic association is a far cry from the benevolence and gentle dignity of the original Atlantean race.

Atlantis in the New World

The evidence presented by the ancient maps appears to suggest the existence in remote times, before the rise of any known cultures, of a true civilization, of an advanced kind, which either was localized in one area but had worldwide commerce, or was, in a real sense, a worldwide culture.

— Charles Hapgood
Maps of the Ancient Sea Kings (1966)

Architects, statesmen, and lawmakers of the New World were often as obsessed with the symbols of Atlantis as those of the Old World. For instance, our nation's most important landmark is built upon *a hill* (i.e., Capitol Hill), with a stone wall that surrounds its border. Key governmental landmarks and structures are in the vicinity of this central hill, which is planted with hundreds of species of trees, bushes, and flowers. In springtime it is a lush and almost paradisiacal botanical garden reminiscent of the gardens of Atlantis City. The designs of the Capitol's dome and its grounds were fashioned to resemble the classic architecture of the Old World, thus pointing back to the legacy of Acropolis Hill.

Inside the dome we find a huge atrium that connects the House and Senate buildings. Completed in 1824, the rotunda is the symbolic and physical heart of the United States Capitol. Six groups of figures were painted around the perimeter of the canopy, and, according to the office of the Architect of the Capitol, the paintings variously depict:

1.   *"War,"* with the armed goddess Freedom and the eagle defeating Tyranny and Kingly Power.

2.   *"Science,"* with the goddess Minerva teaching Benjamin Franklin, Robert Fulton, and Samuel F. B. Morse.

3.   *"Marine,"* with Neptune/Poseidon holding his trident and Venus/Aphrodite holding the transatlantic cable.

4. *"Commerce,"* with Mercury handing a bag of money to Robert Morris, the financier of the American Revolution.

5. *"Mechanics,"* with Vulcan/Hephaestus at the anvil and forge, producing a cannon and a steam engine.

6. *"Agriculture,"* with Ceres seated on the McCormick Reaper, accompanied by America in a red liberty cap and Flora picking flowers.

Figure 4:3
The architectural motif of the Capitol in Washington, D.C., is reminiscent of the Acropolis Hill.

Figure 4:4
Statue of the goddess Liberty stands atop the Capitol dome in Washington, D.C.

Figure 4:5
The Statue of Liberty stands on a walled, circular island.
The structure is reminiscent of the terraced Acropolis Hill
on Atlantis, with the goddess at the summit.

Figure 4:6
The "Goddess of Knowledge," Minerva (Greek Athena), in the
eye of the dome of the Capitol rotunda. She is shown giving
scientific knowledge to Benjamin Franklin, Robert Fulton, and
Samuel F.B. Morse. Poseidon is seen to the left, and George
Washington is shown rising to the heavens on top right.

These mythological figures hark back to the gods of Rome, of Greece before that, then further back to the deities of the Egyptians, and beyond that to the Sumerian gods. They truly emanate from a prehistoric era. Even in these depictions in the Capitol rotunda, these godlike figures instruct humanity in the arts of civilized life, not unlike Plato's description of the Atlantean gods. The legends and images of these gods once uniformly adorned the palaces and temples of the world's greatest civilizations; Atlantean structural motifs seem to govern the designs of their sacred and public buildings. And to this day, thousands of years later, they are etched in the heart of the most important building of one of the world's most powerful nations.

5

Treasure Hunt

*Such, then, are the traditional theories, and it looks
as if the statements of their advocates were in manifest
conflict. But the reason of this conflict is that each group
is in fact stating a part, whereas they ought to have
taken a comprehensive view of the subject as a whole.*

— Aristotle
On Generation and Corruption (350 B.C.)

To those who are unfamiliar with the original story as it appears
in Plato's writings, the mention of Atlantis may conjure visions
of mermaids and ancient kings living in an underwater city. What
was once valued as true history and religiously handed down
by our ancient ancestors has, sadly, become a popular fairy tale
fit for Disney cartoons, New Age revelations, and the weekly
tabloids. This commercialization and exploitation of Plato's story
for questionable purposes has muddied the waters for earnest
research. With no real standards of scholarship, new Atlantis
theories are too often spun out into the channels of the media
without sufficient regard for the justification of their claims.
The problem is further compounded by often legitimate but
unsuccessful expeditions in search of the island, archeological
treasure hunts that so far have unfortunately led nowhere. All
this manner of activity has given Atlantis a severe case of over-
exposure. Yet the story remains so compelling, and its longevity

so remarkable, that there seems no end to the theories and speculation about the lost continent.

The central problem with Atlantis research, as I have pointed out, is this: Researchers have raked through Plato's numerous clues over the centuries, but each new theory ignores a majority of the Greek philosopher's very concrete markers. Even the leading current theories that have produced best-selling books are based on a small and arbitrary subset of these crucial indicators. Those who have carefully studied Plato's own words know that the bulk of existing Atlantis theories have little to do with the details he provided. They know that Plato's text has all too often been misappropriated from its context.

The second great difficulty with previous research is harder to pinpoint, but still essential: Any claim to have found a great civilization—indeed the very origin of civilization—must make sense on a variety of levels other than the literary criteria of Plato's clues. In short, any credible Atlantis theory must map well to what is known about world mythology and the history of civilization. It must be plausible in that context as well.

And finally, scientific developments in recent years allow us to add one more element: Any acceptable theory must be consistent with modern geology and geophysics, and in doing so should make use of the best of today's research techniques—for example, the latest technology and software that permits us to examine and map the ocean floor.

In the past few hundred years alone, researchers have pointed to Crete, Thera, Troy, Malta, Spain, Scandinavia, Sweden, Germany, the North Sea, the Azores Islands, the Canary Islands, the Bimini Islands, Cuba, the Bermuda Triangle, Bolivia, Brazil, the Middle East, Indonesia, the Sahara Desert, and even Antarctica. It is not in our interest to review in detail the work of every researcher who has pointed to a particular location; there are literally dozens of books currently on the market that review the various theories, books, and expeditions in intimate detail. Our aim instead will be to examine the principles that underlie the most recent popular theories, and to contrast them with Plato's descriptions and our own additional criteria. And it will be shown that not a single one of these theories regarding the supposed locations of Atlantis has merit.

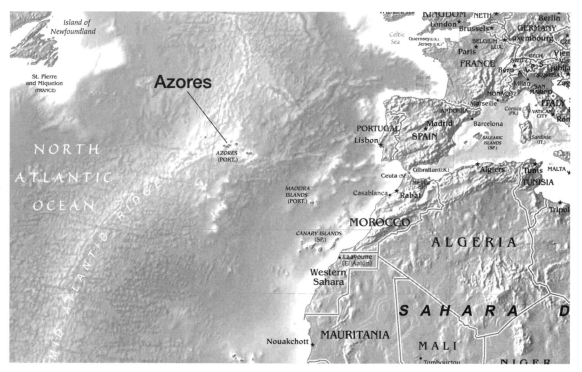

Figure 5:1
For over a century, the Azores Islands have been considered as the possible location of Atlantis.

The Azores

The Azores are a grouping of nine major islands owned by Portugal that are located in the North Atlantic Ocean. Because they lie about one thousand miles directly west of the European continent, the Azores are a logical candidate for Atlantis because they are "opposite the Pillars of Hercules." (This notion assumes, of course, that Plato's reference is synonymous with the Strait of Gibraltar.) Situated over the Mid-Atlantic Ridge, these islands are geologically unstable, experiencing numerous earthquakes and volcanic eruptions. Not unlike Plato's account, the Azores rise sharply from rocky shores to heights reaching over 7,000 feet; further, they enjoy a subtropical climate, vast forests, abundant flora, and agricultural produce that includes cereals, fruits, and vegetables. There were even hot springs on the islands, conforming to yet another one of Plato's clues.

Sitting literally opposite the Strait of Gibraltar and in the Atlantic Ocean, it is no wonder that so many people pointed to this region as the home of the Atlantean race. Ignatius Donnelly wrote extensively about his belief that the Azores and Canary Islands were indeed Atlantis: "The Azores Islands are undoubtedly the peaks of the mountains of Atlantis. They are even yet the centre of great volcanic activity. They have suffered severely from eruptions and earthquakes."[1]

When Donnelly published his book about Atlantis in 1882, the world had just begun to gather observations about the Atlantic Ocean. The British Admiralty and the Royal Society conducted extensive tests of the ocean in the 1800s from 362 stations, with 492 deep soundings and 133 dredgings. The *Report on the Scientific Results of the Voyage of H.M.S. Challenger* was issued in 50 volumes between 1880 and 1895 with analysis of the ocean temperature, its currents, depths, and contours of the basins as well as various biological investigations. This exciting direction of scientific study gave hope to many that the long-awaited discovery of Atlantis was at hand. Many researchers eagerly adopted Donnelly's theory.

Even as late as 1997, geologists were still suggesting that Atlantis may have sunk into the earth's liquid magma, leaving its mountaintops as the Azores Islands. Those who hold to the Azores theory generally believe that these islands once formed part of a much greater landmass that sank beneath the waves and is now thousands of feet below the surface of the ocean.

Figure 5:2
The scientific research conducted aboard the *H.M.S.
Challenger* in the late 19th century is considered to be
the beginnings of modern oceanography.

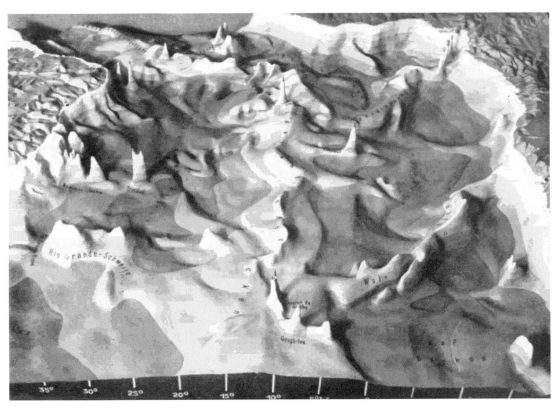

Figure 5:3
One of the earliest 3D models of the Mid-Atlantic Ridge made from observations
on board the German research vessel *Meteor* between 1925 and 1927.

However, there are serious problems with the Azores hypothesis. Chief among these is the islands' distance from the European continent. As noted, the Azores Islands are a thousand miles to the west, with no land bridge. This makes it difficult to explain how humans could have reached the islands in prehistoric times. Indeed, when the Azores were first discovered in 1427, there was no evidence of any previous human or animal habitation or even visitation on any of the islands. No archeological evidence has ever been found on the Azores—and no sign of an indigenous culture. Surely, if these were the remains of Atlantis, there would have to be some legacy of the lost civilization, since it supposedly had extensive trade relations with neighboring nations. But in *Lost Atlantis: New Light on an Old Legend* (1969), J.V. Luce seems to put the question to rest: "There never was an Atlantic land bridge since the arrival of man in the world: there is no sunken landmass in the Atlantic; the Atlantic Ocean must have existed in its present form for at least a million years."[2]

In *Atlantis Destroyed* (1988), Rodney Castleden reaffirmed Luce's contention that the story of Atlantis cannot be corroborated by any natural phenomena occurring in the Atlantic Ocean:

> Long-lived upward-moving plumes of material in the mantle push the mid-ocean ridge up so that in places it breaks the surface of the ocean. Volcanoes that are active while located over the plumes move gradually sideways and down into the ocean basins as on slow-moving conveyor belts: they become extinct as they leave the crest of the ridge. There is no sudden submergence: the processes are gradual and slow. Inspection of the ocean floor shows that Donnelly's connecting ridges do not exist, at any depth.[3]

More importantly, it is a known fact today that ocean levels do not fluctuate to great degrees for any reason; neither the melting of the glaciers at the end of the last ice age, nor a powerful tsunami could have washed over the islands with such drastic speed and violence as described in the *Critias*. The melting of glaciers happens slowly and is hardly noticeable. Tsunamis, likewise, while capable of traveling at great speeds under water (up to 400 mph), are barely noticed on the surface in open waters. Ocean research has shown that tsunamis only reach dangerous heights when they approach a continental shelf. These facts point to the conclusion that the cataclysmic flooding described by Plato could not have happened to the Azores.

In the final analysis, any credible claim of the discovery of Atlantis will need more supporting evidence than the mere presence of hot springs, volcanoes, high mountains, and tectonic plates. Plato's fifty characteristics—plus the many other clues I have assembled from archeological, mythological, and historical data—add up to a specific picture. The Azores Islands support very few of these indicators, and they are simply not a part of our ancient cultural history. Neither are they located in an area that may be considered as supporting prehistoric dynasties.

Needless to say, in time the Azores theory sank below the waves of public opinion.

The Americas

Few people realize how powerful the myth of Atlantis has been in shaping world events, including the very discovery of America. When Columbus first set sail into the unknown expanses of the Atlantic Ocean, he entertained the possibility that Atlantis might be located somewhere opposite the Strait of Gibraltar.

By this time in the late fifteenth century, the Azores theory was already part of Atlantis lore. In Columbus's possession was a geographical treatise by Cardinal Pierre d'Ailly called *Imago Mundy*, which suggested that the "terrestrial paradise perhaps is the place which the authors call the Fortunate Islands [i.e., the Canary Islands]." But Columbus pushed forward far beyond the Azores and Canary Islands. His small fleet continued into uncharted waters in search of true Atlantis and, at the same time, on the lookout for India.

Columbus first stumbled upon an island in the Bahamas. As he explored the region, he did not abandon his belief in Atlantis. He sent letters from the New World to King Ferdinand and Queen Isabella describing the beautiful islands with their lush and fertile plains, tropical weather, friendly natives, vast rivers, abundant foods, and precious metals. These letters to the royal couple contained hints that he might be nearing the location of Atlantis.

Predictably, soon after his exploration of the new continent, Spanish commentators began to propose that North America, South America, and indeed the Americas as a whole were the equivalent of Plato's Atlantis. Of course, this theory ignored Plato's clear indication that Atlantis was an island from which one could access "the whole opposite continent"; thus, an entire continent itself could hardly be considered a candidate.[4] But this obvious problem did not seem to prevent many prominent thinkers, including Sir Francis Bacon, from concluding that the island of Atlantis had at last been found.

The proponents of the Americas theory assume that Solon's reference to the Pillars of Hercules is synonymous with the Strait of Gibraltar—a notion that, as pointed out earlier, seems to be based on an arbitrary interpretation of Solon's statement. Although the major civilizations of Solon's day had barely ventured outside the Strait of Gibraltar, we are expected to believe that the Egyptians knew not only about the Azores and the archipelago of the Bahamas, but also about the American continent itself thousands of miles to the west. The Egyptian records of Atlantis were reportedly handed down for thousands of years prior to Solon's time; that fact alone renders it most unlikely that these extremely ancient societies were producing world maps and utilizing global navigational systems.

Despite these logical problems, the Americas thesis has survived to this day. In more recent times, many people have pointed to the Caribbean Islands themselves, as well as the Bimini Islands, as likely sites. The Biminis are a string of islands in the northwestern Bahamas extending forty miles north to south, and resting fifty miles east of Florida. Today, the main island, North Bimini, attracts tourists to its beaches and contains many yacht harbors. Were it not for a series of predictions from the well-known psychic Edgar Cayce, this would seem an unlikely spot to look for Atlantis. A firm believer in Atlantis, Cayce envisioned it

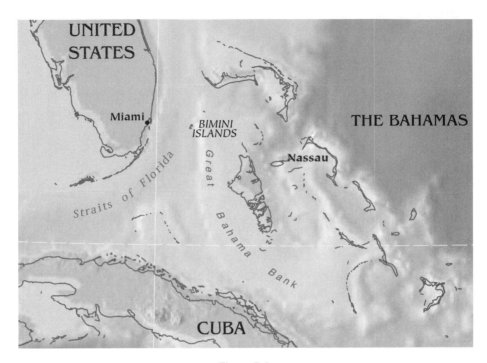

Figure 5:4.
The famed psychic Edgar Cayce once predicted that
Atlantis would resurface in the area of the Bimini Islands,
which are situated to the east of the Florida coast.

as "an enormous ocean-bound landmass that stretched from the Bahamas and Caribbean across to the West Coast of Africa."[5]

To accept the so-called Bimini hypothesis requires us to buy into the notion that Cayce's predictions were completely reliable; there is really no other good reason. But Cayce's Atlantis offers very few matches to the fifty clues presented in chapter 3, and even more conspicuous is the absence of any geologic indicators that a landmass of such dimensions ever existed.

Whatever one may think of building theories around psychic visions, the fact is Cayce's predictions have not proven to be reliable. For example, Cayce claimed to have foreseen the destruction of Los Angeles, San Francisco, and New York, as well as the sliding of much of Japan into the sea sometime between 1958 and 1998. Most notably, he also predicted that portions of Atlantis would rise again in the late 1960s. As the appointed time approached, this claim created a whirlwind of controversy that prompted a number of his followers to conduct several research expeditions to the region—just to make sure. In *Atlantis: The Autobiography of a Search* (1970), Robert Ferro and Michael Grumley recount their adventure:

> We had both read Cayce's prediction that signs of Atlantis would appear in the Bahamas, probably off Bimini, in either 1968 or 1969. We had been interested, I probably slightly more than Robert, in what form these signs would take, and in what type of impact they would create. ... And thinking about taking a boat, about which we had not a shred of knowledge, into an area we knew absolutely nothing about, in the hopes of finding some remnant of a civilization which hadn't been heard from for eleven and a half thousand years. It is no small wonder that our friends thought the idea quixotic at best, and, at worst, the very zenith of lunacy.[6]

The anticipation, strange as it was, actually did lead to something worth investigating. During a routine flight between Miami and Nassau in 1968, Captain Robert Brush and co-pilot Trigg Adams spotted what looked like a J-shaped road under the clear, shallow waters. It was comprised of a series of large stones, seemingly laid out like a pavement for a road heading in an east-west direction, almost a third of a mile in length and relatively far from shore. Press releases were dispatched from Miami announcing that an ancient temple had been found and that all of it is "definitely man-made." Predictably, the scientific world scoffed at the theory and brushed it off as a pile of loose rocks. Eventually, even the believers had to concede that "the Road was a completely natural formation, down which no lost civilization, naked or clothed, had ever wandered or danced."[7]

As seen in the video documentary *Calypso's Search for Atlantis* (1978), Jacques Cousteau conducted his own search for Atlantis in the Aegean Sea while his son, Philippe, investigated the J-shaped Bimini road, the Coco Islands, the Azores, and elsewhere. Their investigations led nowhere, sadly, with Jacques exclaiming at one point that a broken Minoan cup found off the shores of Thera was "the most important" discovery of the whole trip. In short, this was another attempt to find something, anything, that could be tied to the Atlantis legend, but in the end it proved to be little more than a few stones lying in shallow waters.

Bolivia

The search continues to this day in the Americas, and the theory *du jour* now places Atlantis in Bolivia. As reviewed earlier, the Bimini theory relies mainly on psychic predictions, and to some extent Plato's mention of the "other island" that led to the opposite continent. But it offers few relevant matches to the physical description of Atlantis. The Bolivian theory, on the other hand, concentrates mainly on the physical dimensions of Atlantis while ignoring practically everything else. It is difficult, to put it mildly, to believe that a nation on the western edge of South America, and bordering the Pacific Ocean, could correlate at all with Plato's story of Atlantis.

Nevertheless, this theory has recently been proposed by J.M. Allen, a former British intelligence officer in his recent book *Atlantis: The Andes Solution*. The Bolivia hypothesis points to a semirectangular plain that is over 12,000 feet above sea level. It is not on an island, nor is it submerged in water, and yet we are told that this distant land situated many thousands of miles from even the Atlantic coast of America was the homeland of the Atlanteans. Allen attempts to relate this location to Plato's account by showing that the area in question did indeed experience flooding about 9000 B.C. The theory is supposedly further corroborated by the facts that the plain is surrounded by mountains that contain gold, silver, copper, and tin; has a low hill close to the sea; and is prone to volcanic and earthquake activity.

The Bolivian theory perfectly illustrates the inevitable errors that arise from taking parts of Plato's story out of context and applying them to various regions in the world, without paying attention to the overall themes of the Atlantis legend. Basing most of one's claim on merely finding a plain that seems to match Plato's description of the great plain of Atlantis is simply not enough. The case might be strengthened, for example, if Bolivia were an island! It would also be more convincing if this plain were not 12,000 feet above sea level; such a scenario would seem to make the central city of Atlantis rather difficult as an accessible port of entry for ships at sea. Also unexplained is how the armies of Atlantis were supposed to have reached Egypt all the way from Bolivia!

What could possibly explain the development of an intimate relationship of a nation on the far side of South America with Egypt or any Mediterranean civilization? In addition to a complete absence of archeological evidence in Bolivia of an Atlantean civilization, it would seem that the distance factor alone would invalidate the Bolivian hypothesis. Every practical consideration suggests that cultures separated by thousands of miles of ocean, and thousands of years time before commercial air travel, would develop in nearly complete isolation from each other.

Antarctica

In the search for Atlantis, it seems that no theory is too revolutionary to be considered, even if it requires the whole crust of the

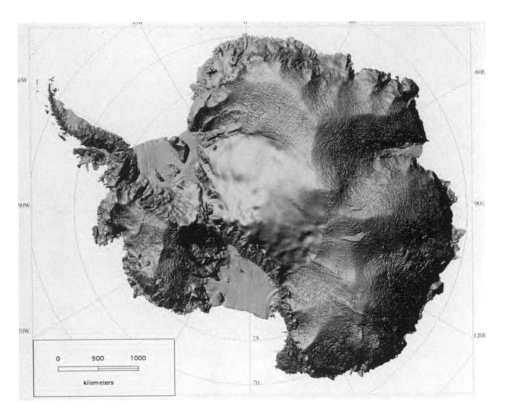

Figure 5:5
Recent theories suggest that the Antarctica landmass was once closer
to the equator and was possibly the original location of Atlantis.

planet to be displaced thousands of miles in order for things to make sense. Thus, another relatively modern theory equates the island of Atlantis with Antarctica. This odd hypothesis proposes that the frigid landscape of the Antarctic was formerly tropical because the landmass was once much closer to the equator. The theory suggests that a massive cataclysm caused the whole surface crust of our planet to shift, causing the landmass to migrate to where it is today.

The Antarctica hypothesis first appeared in the 1950s through the work of Charles H. Hapgood in his book *Earth's Shifting Crust: A Key to Some Basic Problems of Earth Science* (1958). A professor of the history of science at Keene College in New Hampshire, Hapgood developed an original notion he called Earth Crust Displacement (ECD). The late professor studied numerous

Renaissance and early-modern maps of the world and made the startling observation that some of the maps seemed to depict a southern landmass similar to Antarctica—but one that was much closer to the equator. He proposed that this landmass was none other than the island of Atlantis, which subsequently shifted toward the polar region and iced over.

Hapgood's theory gained much credence due to his lengthy correspondence (170 pages of letters) with Albert Einstein, which led to a glowing foreword by the famed physicist for Hapgood's book. Einstein wrote: "In a polar region there is continual deposition of ice, which is not symmetrically distributed about the pole. The earth's rotation acts on these irregularly deposited masses, and produces centrifugal momentum that is transmitted to the rigid crust of the earth. The constantly increasing centrifugal momentum produced in this way will, when it has reached a certain point, produce a movement of the earth's crust over the rest of the earth's body. . . ."[8]

Although it has never been taken seriously in academic circles, writers like Graham Hancock (*Fingerprints of the Gods,* 1995) and Flem-Ath (*When the Sky Fell: In Search of Atlantis,* 1997) have continued to propound this hypothesis with the aid of quasi-scientific methods. The basic notion of ECD is that the earth's lithosphere, which is composed of individual plates, at times moves as a whole over the asthenosphere, or, as Hancock puts it: ". . . much as the skin of an orange, if it were loose, might shift over the inner part of the orange all in one piece."[9]

This theory moves from Hapgood's interpretations of old world maps, which are suspect at best, to suggest the incredible notion that Antarctica was located 30 degrees further north about 12,000 years ago. Hapgood cited climatalogical, paleontological, and anthropological evidence to support his idea that some land masses moved toward the tropics while others moved toward the poles, with catastrophic results for the inhabitants of the world.

In other words, whereas today's geophysicists now know that the shifting of tectonic plates happens randomly and over a period of millions of years, ECD suggests that the crust of the earth shifted in one piece and over a period of only a few hundred years. We are thus led to the conclusion that Plato's story of Atlantis originated with this huge shift in the earth's crust, which precipitated tremendous seismic and volcanic activity as well as the melting of the former ice caps, causing the masses of the population to seek higher ground to avoid an ocean in upheaval. Of course, the scientific world at large has mostly ignored these theories as fables. Geologists tell us that Antarctica has been frozen for millions, if not hundreds of millions of years.

It is difficult to see how such a theory could be entertained as the solution to the Atlantis puzzle; nevertheless, it has created some media interest and produced several books. Numerous documentaries have covered the Atlantis mystery, incorporating the Antarctica thesis as yet another possible clue to the disappearance of Atlantis, all without a single match to Plato's description. Supposedly, future research and satellite imagery will one day lead to the discovery of the once-tropical island, now buried far beneath the frozen landmass, or perhaps the shining city will one day resurface when another shift in the earth's crust will undo the glacial damage.

Unless we literally turn the world on its head we have virtually nothing to substantiate this theory; it demands not only the stretching of the imagination but also the crust of the earth itself. Unfortunately, forcing its pieces where they do not belong cannot solve the Atlantis jigsaw puzzle—the big picture must make sense, based on the match to Plato's description and the many related factors we have presented.

The Mediterranean Sea

Who can make the muddy water clear?
Let it be still, and it will gradually become clear.

— Lao-Tzu
Tao-te Ching (600 B.C.)

Among the believers, Atlantology is divided between two primary groups: Those who believe that Atlantis was inside the Mediterranean and those who believe that it was outside, somewhere beyond the Strait of Gibraltar. The reason so many researchers naturally focus their attention on the Mediterranean instead of the Atlantic is the overwhelming evidence for the Mediterranean as the cradle of civilization. With its indications of written languages, scientific development, political evolution, and formal education—not to mention myths and symbols that correlate to Plato's account—the Near East seems the most practical and logical consideration for being the host of the Atlantis civilization. After all, the legend of Atlantis itself was a *product* of the Mediterranean peoples.

Although prehistoric ruins and megalithic sites have been found scattered throughout the Mediterranean region, the greatest concentration of evidence was found in the Near East. Indeed, the ancient civilizations of South America, Asia, Europe, and Africa reflect a small amount of Atlantean legacy, but Atlantis itself was more than a few megalithic structures in far-flung areas. If we see the story within the context of its prehistoric legacy throughout the world, Atlantis must be regarded as the source and center of all civilization.

Still, there is nothing in the *Critias* that would definitively prove that Atlantis was either in the Mediterranean or the Atlantic. This is due to four central problems which we will briefly review:

1. Our incomplete knowledge of ancient geography.
2. Semantic errors by interpreters (possibly including Solon and/or Plato himself).

Figure 5:6
The Mediterranean Sea and surrounding mainland.

3. Inevitable mistranslations.

4. Inherent contradictions within the *Critias.*

The first problem poses a significant challenge to us. We know that the ancients' notion of the world was drastically different from ours, consisting only of lower Europe, northern Africa, and portions of the Near and Middle East. Surrounding this relatively small, circular land area was a vast ocean they called the Atlantic. The Atlantic, therefore, was not confined to the western portion of the Mediterranean but also surrounded the southern, northern, and eastern portion of their world. It is reasonable to suppose that to the ancients, the Mediterranean region itself would have seemed like an immense area, nearly as difficult to navigate as interplanetary travel is for us today. The Mediterranean Sea's sole gateway to the Atlantic Ocean, the Strait of Gibraltar, is bounded to the north by the Rock of Gibraltar, which was once crowned with silver columns by Phoenician mariners to indicate the limits of safe travel for ancient sailors.

To an ancient Egyptian, therefore, the Mediterranean was practically the whole world. If the Egyptians of Solon's time knew virtually nothing about the Atlantic Ocean, and were perpetuating a story that was passed down for many thousands of years, then how can anyone expect to find geographical accuracy in their account? To point to places like Bolivia, America, Indonesia, or Australia as possible locations for Atlantis is a mistake that only someone from the modern era can make, for no Egyptian of Solon's time would be aware of the existence of these lands, much less know specific and intricate details about them. It would be like expecting someone from our generation to know the topography of a planet from another solar system.

Can anyone believe that the native merchants of Greece and other ancient empires who traded with, learned from, and even lived on Atlantis had all traveled back and forth to an island that was outside the Mediterranean and thousands of miles away? A more reasonable proposal would be that, if Atlantis ever existed, its remains would be somewhere in close proximity to the seat of these ancient empires who also bear the mark of Atlantean culture and art.

The second problem stems from semantic errors and is clearly outlined in the *Critias* itself. Solon stated that the Egyptians had translated the legend of Atlantis to their own Egyptian tongue from the original Atlantean language. He also stated that he translated it again to his native Greek. Each time these translations took place, the names of the central characters and places were likewise changed. Plato wrote about this problematic feature of the Atlantis story:

> Solon intended to use the story in his own poem. And when, on inquiring about the significance of the names, he learned that the Egyptians had translated

the originals into their own language, he went through
the reverse process, and as he learned the meaning of
a name wrote it down in Greek.[10]

This unfortunate changing of names injected much confusion and error into the story. It explains, for instance, why the word "Atlantis" is not found before Plato's time; this is the case not because the story of Atlantis did not exist, as many researchers erroneously assume, but rather because this was the first time the Greek name for the island is found in history.

As reviewed previously, we find the legend of Atlantis in some of the oldest extant historic texts. The original Egyptian name for Atlantis was Keftiu, one of the four pillars of the world on which the sky rested, according to the Egyptians, and the root of the modern word "capital." Keftiu is commonly accepted to be either the island of Crete or Cyprus, which, in either case, points to the eastern Mediterranean Sea and not the Atlantic Ocean. And since the Egyptians had translated the original name of the island to their own native tongue and renamed it Keftiu, a generic term, then it is fair to say that we really do not know the true name of Atlantis.

Clearly, with all the inherent linguistic problems and geographical contradictions associated with this most ancient of world tales, we can see that any definitive statement from Atlantologists who claim that Atlantis *must* be in the Atlantic Ocean is at best questionable. Practical reason suggests, at least at this juncture, that claims of proof should be avoided, for we simply cannot know for sure. But we do have, and must rely on, the accumulating scientific data and the clues to be found in the *Timaeus* and *Critias*.

The third problem is a basic translation issue. In *Atlantis Destroyed* (1998), Rodney Castleden wrote about the possibility of a very simple translation error that would have easily thrown anyone off track in the search for Atlantis:

Solon's original text may nevertheless have read not 'μειζων' but, 'μεσου' meaning a 'middle point between Libya and Asia' (i.e., between Africa and Anatolia), which describes the location of Crete perfectly. . . . Plato may have felt that the huge dimensions Solon gave for Atlantis meant that the description 'midway between Libya and Asia' had to be a mistake and altered the text accordingly. Plato assumed that Solon's pen had slipped. It is nevertheless clear from the climate—warm wet winters and hot dry summers (Crit. 118e)—that Atlantis must have occupied a location within the Mediterranean basin; the significance of this detail is usually overlooked.[11]

The correction of this potential mistake would place the location of Atlantis, again, in the eastern Mediterranean Sea "between Libya and Turkey," not in the Atlantic Ocean. Castleden observed that this point is further corroborated by the fact that Plato's description of Atlantis's climate involves warm wet winters and hot dry summers, which simply do not exist in the Atlantic Ocean but do precisely match the weather patterns of the eastern Mediterranean.

The final reason for our focus on the Mediterranean as the most likely spot to find Atlantis is that the Atlantic theory simply does not fit within the general context of the story. In *Unearthing Atlantis: An Archaeological Odyssey* (1991), Dr. Charles Pellegrino wrote about the description of the Atlantean empire and the peculiar direction in which its power grew to surrounding lands: "For a civilization said to be coming out of the Atlantic, the pattern of conquest is strange, moving, according to Plato, from the eastern Mediterranean shores of Greece, Libya, and Egypt to the rest of the Mediterranean—toward, not from, Gibraltar—with no mention of conquest in northern Spain or along the Atlantic shores of Africa. Plato has described a civilization radiating out of the eastern central Mediterranean, from the direction of Minoan Crete."[12]

There is indeed no mention of Atlantean conquests in the western Mediterranean, nor is there the same wealth of archeological, mythological, or historical data to be found in that area of the world. If Atlantis really did exist in the Atlantic and harbored a relatively advanced and altruistic empire that subsequently imparted the gift of civilization to neighboring lands, then why is the seat of the ancient world's empires located around the eastern Mediterranean, and not the western Mediterranean? Why does the title of the "incubator of civilization" belong to the Mediterranean and not the Atlantic, Bolivia, Antarctica, or the Bahamas?

Ignatius Donnelly's personal research led him to believe that Atlantis was somewhere in the Atlantic, but even he could not help but wonder about the Mediterranean. He wrote: "How comes it that all the civilizations of the Old World radiate from the shores of the Mediterranean? The Mediterranean is a *cul de sac,* with Atlantis opposite its mouth. Every civilization on its shores possesses traditions that point to Atlantis. We hear of no civilization coming to the Mediterranean from Asia, Africa, or Europe—from north, south, or west; but north, south, east, and west we find civilization radiating from the Mediterranean to other lands. . . . Plato says, 'the nations are gathered around the shores of the Mediterranean like frogs around a marsh'."[13]

Dr. Zdenek Kukal, a geologist and former director general of the Czech Geological Survey, is another Atlantologist who is convinced about the Mediterranean theory. In his book *Atlantis: In the Light of Modern Research* (1984), he said: "If we are more modest and place Atlantis in the Mediterranean, the whole story becomes, if not more probable, at least less far-fetched. . . . Are we trying, by praising the Mediterranean, to convey the impression that Atlantis really existed and that it belongs in that sea? By no means. Atlantis, as described by Plato, has never been found by anyone anywhere, and it seems that it never will be. But it was the

Mediterranean, with its ancient civilizations, its conflicts, and its tectonic activity, that inspired Plato. It is the Mediterranean, with its sunken harbors and cities, that can still reveal many surprises. Many parts of its floor remain to be explored."[14] Indeed, much of the Mediterranean seafloor remains unexplored and can harbor many surprises, as many marine archeologists will attest.

Dr. Kukal also points to a telltale sign in Plato's text that clearly reveals the likely close proximity of Atlantis to the eastern Mediterranean. Plato said that the fighting armies of the Athenians and the Atlanteans were "swallowed up by the earth" in the eastern Mediterranean region, while Atlantis was simultaneously submerged under water. If Atlantis was in the Atlantic, then how could a disaster in the eastern Mediterranean basin affect it from thousands of miles away, with enough force to sink it? Dr. Kukal wrote: "This passage, taken to its conclusions, is perhaps the most important in proving that Atlantis, if it existed, was located in the Mediterranean rather than in the Atlantic. How could the brave Greek men fall victim to an earthquake somewhere in Greece while at the same time, and presumably by the same earthquake, Atlantis was swallowed far out in the Atlantic? Such coincidence is impossible."[15]

Discrepancies regarding the nature and size of the great flood, as well as further evidence pointing to the Mediterranean, can also be found in sources such as the great Jewish philosopher of the first century, Philo of Alexandria. As noted by Davis Young in *The Biblical Flood* (1995), "Philo also made the intriguing suggestion that the flood was not 'a trifling outpouring of water but a limitless and immense one, which almost flowed out beyond the Pillars of Heracles (the Strait of Gibraltar) and the Great Sea. Therefore the whole earth and the mountainous regions were flooded.' It is difficult to know what to make of this. In one breath he characterizes the cataclysm as 'limitless and immense' and also appears to limit its extent to the Mediterranean Basin."[16]

Let us therefore consider the key elements of the Mediterranean hypothesis: The Mediterranean Sea has dozens of islands. It has the volcanoes, earthquakes, floods, and climate that Plato described. It has the same fertile land, tropical climate, precious metals, and extensive mountain ranges. It is a part and parcel of the Old World that *produced civilization*. For these reasons, perhaps, the most widely accepted Atlantis theory places it in the Aegean Sea, claiming that its remains are to be found somewhere under the coasts of the Aegean archipelago.

Aegean Sea

Interestingly enough, even those researchers who do not believe in the existence of Atlantis often point to the eastern Mediterranean as the most likely place where the so-called myth originated. One of the best-known translators of Plato's *Critias,* Desmond Lee, belonged to the nonbeliever camp and, like many others before him, assigned the story of Atlantis to Plato's imagination.[17] He admitted that the way Plato provided details about the method in which the Atlantis legend was passed on from the Egyptian priests to Solon, then to Dropides, then to Critias's grandfather, and from Critias to his grandson "is chronologically possible," and he went on to say that "I am prepared to go so far as to say that there may be *some* foundation in fact in Plato's tale." As far as the nature and location of the mythical island, however, Lee believed that if the story had any merit at all, it must have been in reference to one of the natural cataclysms that rocked the Mediterranean islands like Thera and Minoan Crete, saying: "The only other expectation which seems

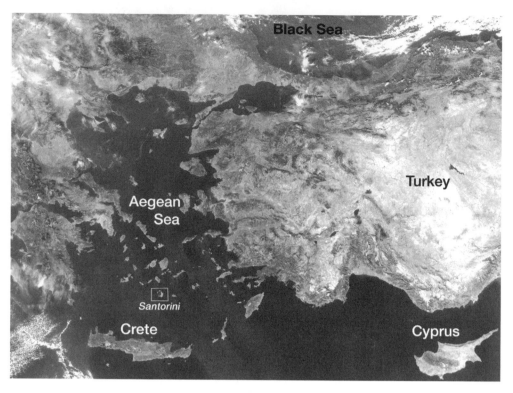

Figure 5:7
The Aegean Sea lies to the west of Cyprus and Turkey. Many writers have
been favorable to the theory that Santorini Island was the site of Atlantis.

reasonable is that the story should have been of a purely Mediterranean disaster in historic times."[18]

Of all the Atlantis theories none is more studied or accepted
by the academic community than one focused in the Aegean, near
the island of Santorini. This hypothesis claims that the legend arose
from the destruction of the island of Thera in connection with a
violent volcanic explosion that rocked the eastern Mediterranean
roughly one thousand years before Plato's time. This event is
known to be one of the most massive volcanic eruptions in history. After the dust settled, there was no longer one island but
three—one of which remains today as the island of Santorini.
Ancient Thera apparently had a sophisticated culture that was
highly influenced by the Minoan civilization on Crete, about

Figure 5:8
One of the most popular theories about the location of Atlantis suggests that the volcanic eruption on the island of Thera, which occured around 1600 B.C., gave birth to the legend about the destruction of the island. This image is an early depiction of how the eruption may have appeared to neighboring peoples.

sixty miles to the south. The city of Akritori, currently under excavation on Santorini, was buried under a layer of ash and pumice much like Pompeii, but without human remains.

The Greek archaeologist Spyridon Marinatos launched the first Akritori excavation project in the 1960s, gradually uncovering the remains of a city that is nearly perfectly preserved. Ancient Akritori presented structures several stories high, decorated with beautiful artwork and relatively modern plumbing systems. Many researchers were encouraged to think that Atlantis was finally found. The impressive culture and sophisticated nature of the

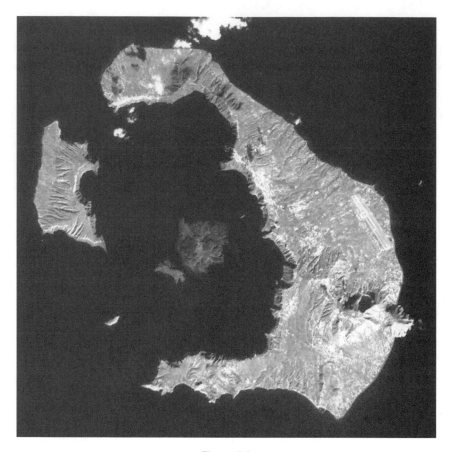

Figure 5:9
The gray spot in the center of this picture was once the volcano
on Thera Island prior to its eruption. This satellite image shows
the present remainder of Thera (Santorini Island).

Minoan civilization as well as its sudden decline after the eruption
of Thera seemed to fit the Atlantis template, and theories were
quickly built around the tsunami that must have originated from
the explosive power of the volcano. Greek authorities encouraged
the hype over the Atlantis connection and as a result Santorini
remains as one of the most popular tourist destinations in the
Aegean today. Even the Atlantis skeptics have entertained the
thought that this may indeed be the source of the great legend. In
Atlantis: The Truth Behind the Legend (1969), A.G. Galanopoulos
wrote:

We have shown that it is not geophysically possible for Atlantis to have been located in the Atlantic; and proved that none of the theories so far advanced to account for its sudden submersion are tenable. We have gone on to indicate that the only logical location must be the Eastern Mediterranean and that the identification of the Pillars of Hercules with the Straits of Gibraltar need not be taken too literally. Finally we have shown that the volcanic activity on a really stupendous scale did take place in the Eastern Mediterranean in the middle of the Bronze Age, and this activity was centered on the island of Santorini, and that it resulted in, among other things, the sudden disappearance of the whole centre of an inhabited, small, round island. The case, therefore, for the identification of Santorini with the Ancient Metropolis of Atlantis is extremely strong, and is supported by a considerable amount of corroborative evidence of very great interest.[19]

Regrettably, no definitive evidence of Atlantis has ever been recovered from Thera that would put the case to rest. The match to Plato is weak in key aspects: For example, there is no trace of a submerged, rectangular plain that is surrounded by mountains. In addition, there is no mention in the *Critias* of a volcanic eruption; as we have seen, Atlantis supposedly sank due to an earthquake and flood. The sinking of the whole of Atlantis, save perhaps its mountainous regions, seems to rule out expectations of finding artifacts on elevated land. Indeed, if the plain of Atlantis were thousands of feet below the mountaintops, there should be an expectation of finding it thousands of feet below the surface of the water.

The most flimsy evidence, however, concerns the estimated date of the eruption. Since the Thera volcano erupted around 1600 B.C., it was necessary to account for the mismatch of time between the sinking of Atlantis and the Thera eruption. In order for Thera to stand as a consistent Atlantis theory, the discrepancy had to be explained as a mistake on the part of Plato, or Solon, or the Egyptian priests. Thera proponents therefore suggested that someone must have erred in transcribing or translating numerals, such that the number 10 was mistaken for 100.

But how probable are such mistakes? Plato said Solon was *told* the story by the Egyptian priest, meaning that Solon was not solely relying on his translation skills of Egyptian numerals. In the *Timaeus,* the Egyptian priest comments to Solon, "The age of our institutions is given in our sacred records as eight thousand years, and the citizens whose laws and whose finest achievements I will now briefly describe to you therefore lived nine thousand years ago. . . ."[20] It seems unlikely that such a mistake in the knowledge of their culture could have been made by a priest, a presumed authority of sacred historical records. At the same time, one need not infer that the Egyptian claim about the actual time period of Atlantis was in fact accurate. Nor can we be sure that the Egyptian beliefs about Atlantean origins and cultural life were correct portrayals. But we are safe in arguing that it is highly improbable that the Egyptian priests were saying something other than what they were reported to have said to Solon. A mistake on Plato's part seems equally unlikely; we know that he was quite aware of the age and legacy of the civilizations around Athens. According to his biographer, Olympiodorus, Plato himself traveled to Egypt and studied sacred science with the high priests of the land, as well as with the Persian Magi in Phoenicia.[21]

The most serious problem with the Thera theory is that the eruption occured around 1600 B.C., while the Atlantis legend, as we have seen, is almost universally understood to predate all recorded history.

The fact remains that Plato's intricate descriptions of the island and its great plain have never been matched to any part of the Aegean seafloor. In short, while the world has benefited much from the archeological and historical investigations that have been initiated from the Thera discovery, there is no bona fide connection with Atlantis.

Many of the arguments advanced in support of Atlantis theories rely solely on their claims being internally consistent while blithely neglecting the necessary factor of correspondence to Plato's account. As we have seen in this chapter, researchers can and have built cases for a discovery of Atlantis by stringing together a number of happenstance observations in ways that, in some superficial respects, are consistent with the original story. However, unless there is a more extensive fit with Plato's clues, and, unless we find a formation on the seafloor corresponding to the described landform that was once above water, these theories lack empirical support and have little scientific merit—let alone credibility based on world history or mythology.

Many people have dedicated much of their lives to investigating what, from a practical standpoint, is no more than a fable. But it may be a mistake to ascribe their efforts to the pursuit of folly. While they may construct, and in some cases, concoct, reckless and wildly divergent interpretations, they have all been captivated by the power of the myth and have acted upon it. While the power of a myth alone is not enough to guarantee its verity, or extra-mythical reality, we might be advised to view such a long-standing belief as the equivalent of smoldering embers, casting smoke and scent into the air. Many of us have caught the scent and are following our senses, believing that "where there's smoke, there must be fire."

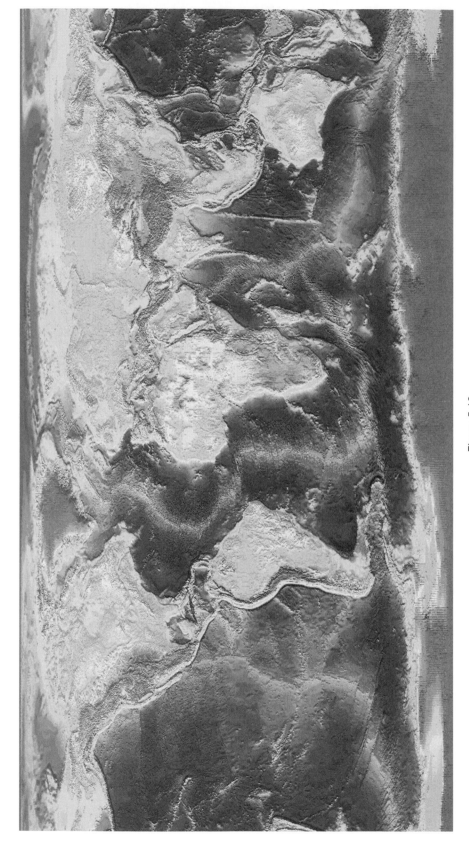

Figure 5:10
Contour map of the world's ocean floors.

Secrets of the Mediterranean Sea

The man who busies himself with the description of the earth
must needs speak, not only of the facts of the present,
but also sometimes of the facts of the past,
especially when they are notable.

— **Strabo**
Geography (1st century B.C.)

The story of Atlantis in Plato's *Timaeus* and *Critias* has generated centuries of confusion because of ambiguities in these texts concerning the *size* and *location* of the island. The rest of Plato's account is relatively unambiguous, leading us to a list of almost fifty reliable clues—some based on simple inferences, and many based on apparent statements of fact.

For example, his descriptions of the physical structure of the island are straightforward. We get a definite picture of the island as it appeared above sea level, allowing some indication of how it might appear on the seafloor today. Other clues come from rational deductions. Plato's description of the tropical climate of Atlantis with its mild winter season and hot dry summers led us to reason that the island could not have been very near to or very far from the equator. Also, his reference to high mountains that protected the lowlands from "cold northerly winds" helped us to infer that the island must have been somewhere in the Northern Hemisphere.

Factual clues and circumstantial items like these have led us a long way, but my selection of Cyprus as the location for Atlantis has been largely guided by Plato's description of the great flood and its consequences, and by new facts about the geologic history of the Mediterranean Sea. In this chapter, I present remarkable scientific evidence that in very ancient times a great flood did indeed rush into the Mediterranean Basin and, in combination with other factors, may have been of the proportions required to actually submerge a mountainous island the size of Plato's Atlantis.

Plato's account of the great flood is so unusual that its rarity aided me in my quest. If this event is taken as a literal description, and not dismissed as poetic exaggeration, then the crucial task must be one of searching for geological conditions in which such a flood *could* have occurred. There are simply very few places in the world where a catastrophe like the one described in the *Critias* is possible. As we reviewed earlier, sudden flooding cannot submerge an island in a vast ocean where there is little average variability in water levels; neither can rising ocean levels due to glacial melting account for this kind of flood. Even powerful tsunamis are barely noticeable in the open expanses of oceans. This leads us to conclude that an inland sea would have to be the more plausible location for such a flood.

Simpler clues also come to our aid in the search process. The destruction of Atlantis involved the nearly complete submergence of a *mountainous* island, which, according to the Egyptians, was one of the highest in the "world." But again, how could a flood submerge the whole of such an island? Consider this quote from the *Timaeus*, in which the Egyptian priests describe events after the Cretans defeated the belligerent Atlantean army *within* the Mediterranean:

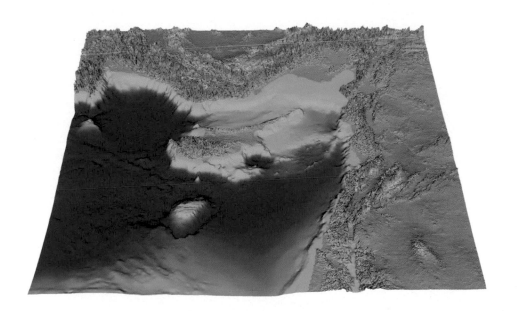

World's first high resolution 3D model of the Eastern
Mediterranean seafloor and surrounding mainland area

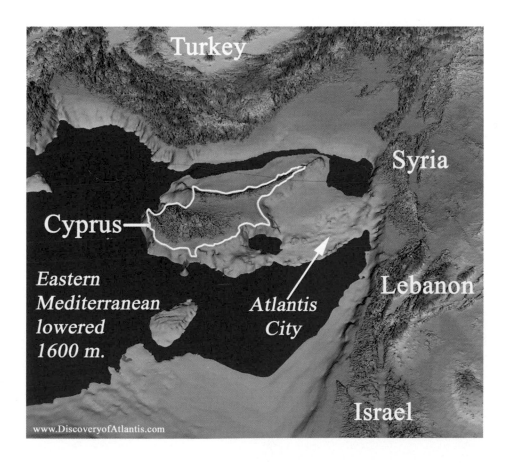

Turkey

Syria

Cyprus

Lebanon

Eastern
Mediterranean
lowered
1600 m.

Atlantis
City

Israel

www.DiscoveryofAtlantis.com

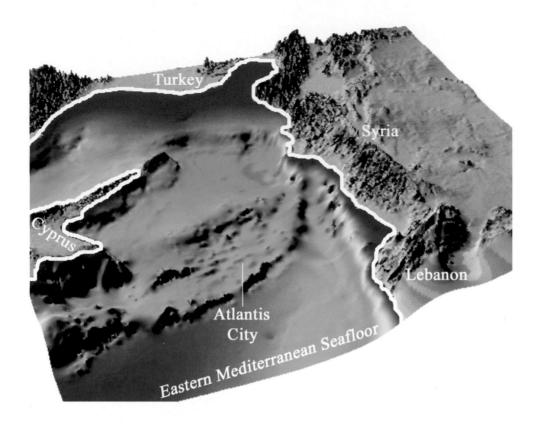

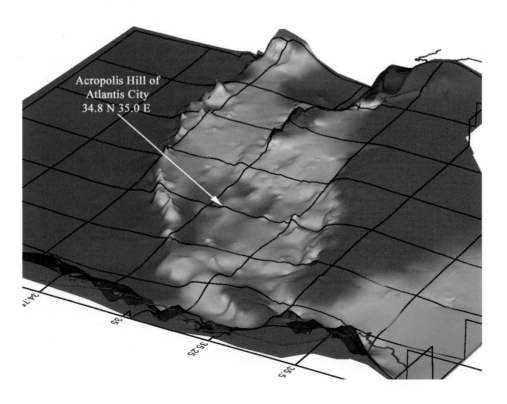

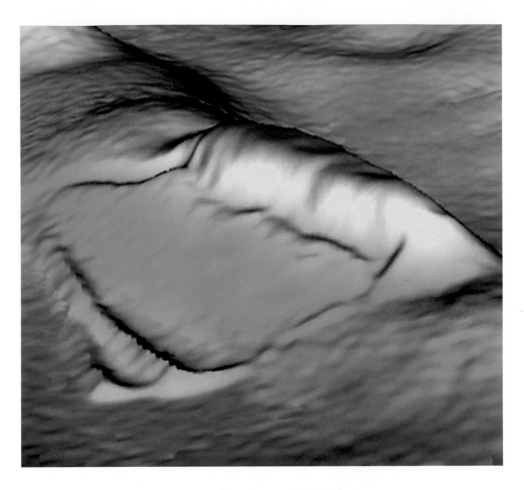

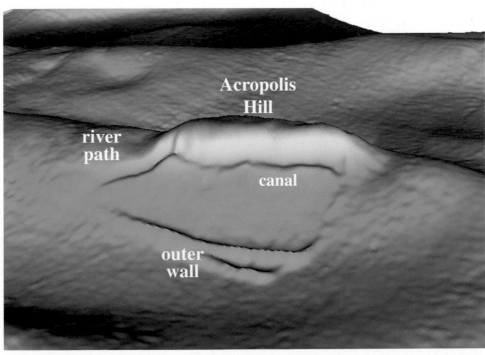

3

EDT vessel
"M/T Flying Enterprise"

From top:
Pre-expedition press conference
Media team on board the ship
Robert and Commodore Bates
Robert and Darios Melas of EDT

5

In the sonar control room with Robert and the Phoenix team, collecting data to generate real-time images of the sea floor.

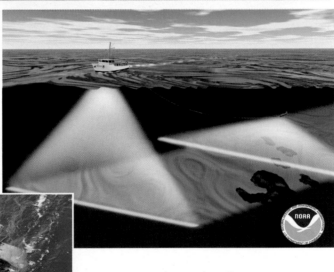

Lowering the
side-scan sonar with
20,000 feet of cable

Sonar Images of the City of Atlantis

Eastern Mediterranean Between Cyprus and Syria
Depth -1500 m (1 mile)

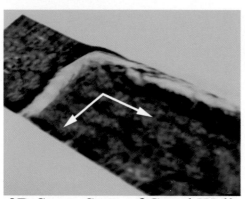

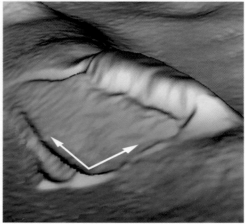

3D Sonar Scan of Canal Wall   Acropolis Hill

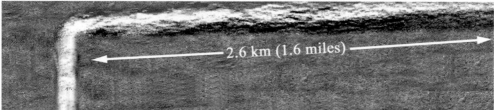

2.6 km (1.6 miles)

Canal Wall Width 100 m (330 ft), Wall Height 10 m (33 ft)

On this island of Atlantis had arisen a powerful and remarkable dynasty of kings, who ruled the whole island, and many other islands as well and parts of the continent; in addition it controlled, within the strait, Libya up to the borders of Egypt and Europe as far as Tyrrhenia. This dynasty, gathering its whole power together, attempted to enslave, at a single stroke, your country and ours and all the territory within the strait....It was then at a later time there were earthquakes and floods of extraordinary violence, and in a single dreadful day and night all your fighting men were swallowed up by the earth, and the island of Atlantis was similarly swallowed up by the sea and vanished; this is why the sea in that area is to this day impassible to navigation, which is hindered by mud just below the surface, the remains of the sunken island.[1]

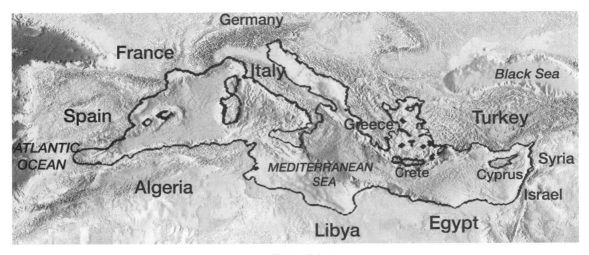

Figure 6:1
Outline of the Mediterranean seafloor.

This section supplies the main visual elements in the Atlantis flood description. Evidently the disaster was one of gigantic proportions and included several different but related natural catastrophes, all of which conspired to bring about the end of the famed island. A combination of "earthquakes and floods of extraordinary violence" pummeled the eastern Mediterranean, and caused the fighting Cretans and Atlanteans to be "swallowed up by the earth," while Atlantis was concomitantly "swallowed up by the sea and vanished." The catastrophe, then, included an earthquake, a flood, and the submergence of land. It is unclear whether the flood was of such proportions that it submerged the whole mountainous island of Atlantis by itself or in combination with land submergence due to the weight of the flood. What is clear is that this was no ordinary flood.

This kind of disaster may indeed be difficult to imagine, but those who are familiar with the unpredictable and volatile geological activity of the Mediterranean will not find it surprising. Here in the warm, tropical climate of the eastern Mediterranean we find the best match for the cultural background of Plato's story, as well as the best match for the complex series of natural disasters that befell Atlantis—the earthquakes, floods, volcanoes, and sinking sea basins are all there.

Historically speaking, islands have been known to rise from the depths of the Mediterranean Sea quite unexpectedly, only to sink again before the neighboring nations have a chance to claim them as their own. For instance, there was an international dispute in 1831 over a small island that appeared in connection with an earthquake, rising from the sea near the strategically desirable Sicilian Channel between Europe and Africa. Britain, France, Spain, and Sicily all laid claim to the tip of this submerged volcano, now known as Graham Island, although in Sicily it was called Ferdinandea, after King Ferdinand II. In *Atlantis: the Antediluvian World,* Ignatius Donnelly refers to this remarkable event, noting that "in about a month the island was two hundred feet high and three miles in circumference."[2] Conflict raged for five months as nations fought over the small island, situated nineteen miles south of Sicily, while visitors climbed to its summit and investors frantically prepared to set up holiday resorts on its beaches. Their high hopes were dashed, however, as the disputed territory sank beneath the surface again, thus extinguishing the little brushfire of nationalist bickering. Interestingly enough,

Graham Island made headlines again in November of 2002 with indications that it was soon to rise again from the depths due to seismic activity associated with the eruption of Mt. Etna.

The Greatest Flood in Human History

The Mediterranean has an unusual history.

— Dr. Kenneth J. Hsu
Challenger at Sea (1992)

The Mediterranean Sea occupies a deep and elongated depression that is nearly landlocked. It is a large, earthquake-prone basin, a deep and wide scar in the earth's crust thousands of feet below the level of the Atlantic Ocean to the west. This ancient sea stretches 2,500 miles from east to west, and an average of 500 miles from north to south, occupying a total area of approximately 970,000 square miles.

The present-day Mediterranean was formed out of the old Tethys Seaway that once existed between the widely separated continents of Africa and Eurasia. As these continents gradually drifted together around thirty million years ago, the slow action of these massive tectonic plates gradually brought the Mediterranean Sea into being. Appropriately, the root words for Mediterranean Sea mean "sea between the lands."

In those far-distant times, the two continental plates began to merge and actually touch one another near the present-day Strait of Gibraltar. In recorded history, this strait has been a narrow channel eight miles in width that connects the Mediterranean to the Atlantic Ocean, but this area has never been geologically stable. It has long been a source of infamous legends and myths. For thousands of years before Columbus charted a course to the New World, this gateway to the Atlantic was considered the edge of the known world to our ancestors. Anyone who ventured outside its borders faced a perilous and uncharted frontier.

However, much evidence points to the likelihood that the Mediterranean was not always connected to the Atlantic by this waterway; at times, the two continental plates were actually connected by a land bridge, completely sealing off the Mediterranean. In *The Atlantis Myth* (1948), H.S. Bellamy noted how ancient geographers "testified that originally the Straits of the Pillars (Strait of Gibraltar) did not exist, but the rock was eventually broken through in a cataclysm."[3] Seismic maps seem to corroborate this theory, indicating the presence of a tremendous focus of earthquake activity around the area of the Strait of Gibraltar. In the scenario suggested by Bellamy, the former land bridge between Spain and Morocco gave way to the Atlantic Ocean—whose waters "poured eastward, in an inconceivably mighty cataract, down into the Mediterranean Basin, which had now sunk below sea level."

Of course, such a violent earthquake, along with the subsequent oceanic flood, would have been catastrophic to the lives and welfare of those ancient peoples then living in the Mediterranean region. Presumably, this would have included the Egyptians, who may have later remembered it in the account given to Solon by the Egyptian priests as "earthquakes and floods of extraordinary violence." The great flood would have filled the Mediterranean Basin and eventually settled to a steady level, but not before the fluctuation of water levels wreaked havoc on the islands and on the coastal cities with their teeming populations.

Though we have ancient records and modern speculations pointing to the possibility of such an extraordinary event, scientific evidence now fully corroborates the story, although not in the

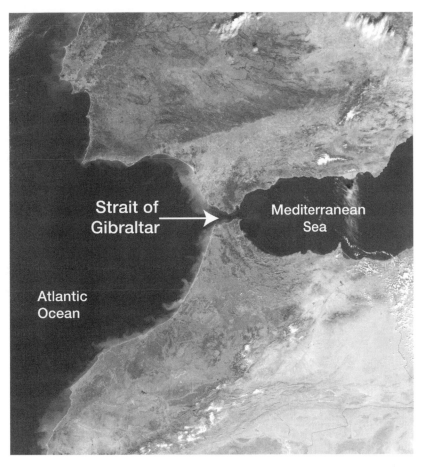

Figure 6:2
Recent scientific research has shown that the Strait of Gibraltar
was once a land bridge which connected Africa to Europe.

time frame described in Plato's account of Atlantis. Nonetheless, geological research proves that the Strait of Gibraltar was indeed once a natural dam that completely separated the Atlantic from the Mediterranean and that the Mediterranean was once a dry valley.[4] In other words, what is now a waterway between the Atlantic Ocean and the Mediterranean Sea was once a narrow land bridge that connected Africa to Europe, leaving the Mediterranean Basin dry in many places. Because of seismic activity, this short isthmus between the two continents collapsed, creating one of the most spectacular and awesome natural events imaginable. The breach of this barrier must have caused an immense waterfall that rushed into the relatively dry Mediterranean basin with such force that it generated a flood of vast proportions. Moreover, evidence shows that such an event must have happened more than once.

The startling scientific proof for such a flood—based on the research presented in this section—has been crucial in developing the case for Cyprus presented in this book.

The first scientific expedition that led to the discovery of the Mediterranean's former state as a dry valley took place in 1970. The funding for the expedition was obtained after sonar studies of the Mediterranean seafloor unexpectedly revealed a hard, sound-reflecting layer 100-200 meters below the bottom; ordinarily, sand, gravel and soft mud are all that should be found on a seabed supposedly as old as that of the Mediterranean. This unexpected discovery of stratification of the sediments led to funding from the National Science Foundation for a drilling project by the *Glomar Challenger,* an amazing vessel equipped with a drilling rig capable of coring samples from the seafloor to a depth of several miles. Little did the pioneering scientists on board this ship realize how their arduous expedition would change the world's understanding of Mediterranean history.

Two well-known and respected geologists shared the position of chief scientists for this effort: Dr. Kenneth Hsu and William Ryan. Hsu was a well-known professor of sedimentology at the Swiss Technical University in Zurich who later became the President of the International Association of Sedimentologists and Chairman of the International Commission on Marine Geology. His book about this remarkable voyage, entitled *The Mediterranean Was a Desert: A Voyage of the Glomar Challenger,* was published in 1983 by Princeton University Press.[5] Bill Ryan is a professor of geology at Columbia University, where he gained much

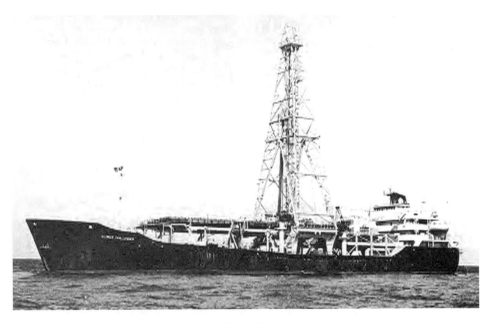

Figure 6:3
The research vessel *Glomar Challenger* was the first in history
to conduct extensive surveys of the Mediterranean seafloor.

notoriety after he co-wrote a popular book with Walter Pitman
entitled *Noah's Flood: the New Scientific Discoveries about the Event
That Changed History* (1999).[6] This book recounts the findings of
the *Glomar Challenger* expedition and how the discoveries led to
the flood theory.[7]

Analyzing the sediments of a seafloor can reveal the sea's
entire history. Ryan writes: "The sedimentary layer of the ocean
floor is a virtual library of information. Its acquisitions are made
of mud, ooze, sand, and rock, with a script choreographed by
climate during the erosion of mountains by precipitation, the
transport of dust from deserts by wind, the wandering of the sea
in meanders of gyres, the freeze and thaw of ice caps, and the life
spans of a multitude of creatures who once colonized the ground,
both wet and dry, and left behind their skeletal remains in the
form of fossils. The texts in this ocean floor library are deciphered
by scientists exploiting the knowledge of physics, chemistry, and
biology."[8]

The core samples of the Mediterranean Basin recovered by Hsu and Ryan revealed that the Mediterranean had been desiccated—and not just once, but possibly several times.[9] They discovered thick layers of minerals such as halite (salt) and gypsum, which are formed when salt water evaporates. In his account of the discovery, Dr. Hsu describes the first moment they realized that a crystallized chunk of salt was part of a sample brought up from the depths of the Mediterranean Sea. The scientists on board actually licked it to make sure their eyes were not playing tricks on them, for salt can only form on the seafloor if all the water has dried up! He wrote: "Ryan, Cita, and I shall perhaps always remember that day as the time we first saw the vision of a salt desert 3,000 meters below the sea level."[10] The salt layers were not just a few dozen meters thick as one would expect if the Mediterranean had dried up just once, but rather several kilometers, suggesting that the basin had repeatedly dried out and then refilled with salt water.

They also found certain fossil shells that one would expect to find only in a shallow salty lagoon or surface evaporation pond, and yet these fossils were found at a depth of over 6,500 feet. Ryan was stunned: "Shallow lagoons on the floor of the Mediterranean Sea? 'No Way!'… the idea seemed absurd even as a preliminary working hypothesis."[11]

But, despite the disbelief of the investigators on board, the evidence now pouring in was painting a clear picture of what had occurred. The Strait of Gibraltar had long ago acted as a kind of natural sea valve, operated by minor, undulating shifts between the African and European continental plates. This activity served to alternately cut off and then later restore the connection between the Mediterranean and the Atlantic Ocean. This finding means that the Mediterranean Sea is essentially an *inlet* of the Atlantic Ocean, whose flow is governed by the Gibraltar gate. The gate is closed when the plates bump together, and open when the plates are "bouncing away" from each other. While the plates are in a collisional phase, the stagnant inlet water begins to evaporate.[12]

The evaporation rate in the Mediterranean Sea is considerable. It is known to be greater than the influx of water entering from rivers around its perimeter. Every time that the continental plates touched at the gate, it was concluded, the now-separated Mediterranean was doomed to evaporate in a matter of 1,000–4,000 years. Such an event is referred to as the Messinian Salinity Crisis. Each time this crisis occurred, it turned a once vast sea into a virtual desert dotted with lakes and lagoons.

The present islands of the Mediterranean would in such periods resemble mountainous plateaus reaching thousands of feet into the air. Even today, if the Strait of Gibraltar were closed off with a great dam, and the sea were again disconnected from the Atlantic Ocean, the Mediterranean would gradually become a dense, salty lake, then a marsh, and finally a desert. The Nile and other rivers that reach the coast from Africa and Europe would plunge for over a mile before reaching the floor of this desert. Studies of the coastal regions of Egypt and Libya have revealed numerous river-cut channels buried at astounding depths. One of these channels cuts into the bedrock at a depth of 4,500 feet!

The Mediterranean Sea, therefore, has a truly remarkable history, and one that we have just begun to understand. As we have seen, the Strait of Gibraltar serves as the gateway between the Atlantic and the Mediterranean, but due to the irregular, back-and-forth shifting of the African and European plates, it serves as a land bridge in one period and a strait in another. What makes this phenomenon so unusual is not the tectonic movement itself, but rather the place of its occurrence and the dramatic geologic effects that follow. And Dr. Hsu suggests that this will probably occur again sometime: "But the days of the beautiful blue sea are numbered. History will likely repeat itself. One can imagine in the not too distant future, say some two or three million years from now, that Gibraltar will be again changed into an isthmus. The Gibraltar falls will be rejuvenated. Cruise ships will be replaced by camel caravans across the new Mediterranean desert."[13]

Bill Ryan explains how the onslaught of proof from various studies eventually washed away his doubts: "More and more evidence poured in. Bone-hunting paleontologists from the American Museum of Natural History in New York discovered some of our very distant primate ancestors in southern Spain. They had come over from Africa, presumably across the barrier that had cut off the Atlantic Ocean from the Mediterranean, and had allowed the latter to dry out. On the island of Cyprus, investigators from University College in London excavated the skeletons of elephants and hippopotamuses from graveyards 5.5 million years old....Apparently they had wandered down a distributary channel of the Nile and deep into the empty desert basin to inhabit lakeside swamps and neighboring savanna."[14] As we have already noted in the list of clues given earlier, the existence of elephant bones on Cyprus provides a direct and remarkable link to Plato's Atlantis story. According to Dr. Hsu, African antelopes and horses galloped across the isthmus of Gibraltar before it was split asunder to become the strait, and the migratory traffic of hippos and elephants from the Nile to Cyprus "might have been more frequent if the wanderers had not had to travel across a desert 2,000 to 3,000 meters below sea level."[15]

Another associate of Dr. Hsu, Gilbert Bocquet of the Botany Institute, found further evidence by researching the origin of the endemic Alpine floras on the coasts of Mediterranean islands like Cyprus and Crete. The only way they could have appeared on these islands was through the desiccation of the Mediterranean before the great deluge.[16] Hsu wrote about the high mountainous plateaus that existed in the Mediterranean Basin before the great deluge that turned them into tiny islands in the present Sea: "Mediterranean islands, such as Corsica and Crete, were 4,000-meter mountain peaks during the Messinian desiccation, and the

Alpine floras on those islands became isolated after the Pliocene deluge...."[17]

The destruction of the Gibraltar dam by earthquake created a disaster of epic proportions for the basin inhabitants, indeed, causing the world's greatest waterfall. As Dr. Hsu puts it in his depiction of the Gibraltar disaster: "Cascading at a rate of 40,000 cubic kilometers per year, the Gibraltar Falls were 100 times bigger than Victoria Falls and a thousand times grander than Niagara. Even with such an impressive influx, it took more than one hundred years to fill the empty Mediterranean. What a spectacle it must have been!"[18] Visualizing a waterfall one thousand times greater than Niagara Falls certainly tests the limits of one's imagination. Like a faucet opening to fill a gigantic bathtub, the incredible torrent of water would have fallen about three miles (three times the depth of the Grand Canyon) and crashed onto the basin before speeding toward the eastern Mediterranean region, traveling at such speeds that anything on its path would have been obliterated.

The final weeks of the *Glomar Challenger* expedition left little ambiguity concerning the implications of the research. There had been an "instantaneous flooding" of a colossal nature that had changed the Mediterranean "from dry salt lake bed to a mile-deep abyss."[19] Is it any wonder that the legend of the great flood is "common to Babylonians, Assyrians, Persians, Egyptians, the city states of Asia Minor, Greece and Italy, and others around the Mediterranean. . . "?[20]

We know now that the Mediterranean was once a vast basin spotted with lakes and lagoons, and that it contained towering plateaus reaching many thousands of feet into the air. We also know that the basin was literally filled in by the greatest flood in human history. This means that Plato's description of the natural disasters that destroyed Atlantis may well have been based on factual events. The new scientific discoveries about the natural history of the Mediterranean directly corroborate the disasters depicted in *Timaeus* and *Critias*.

On the other hand, it must be noted that the Ryan and Hsu data place the desiccation of the Mediterranean at the beginning of the Pliocene Epoch, some five million years ago, long before any humans could have inhabited the great Mediterranean valley. Thus, it was impossible for them to imagine that this awesome flood could have been seen by any humans that subsequently transmitted the story to later generations. No one, according to their preliminary surveys, could have actually seen the great flood.

For this reason, Ryan and Pitman focused their attention on the Black Sea as the most likely candidate for the flood story in the *Gilgamesh Epic*, which they claim was later recounted in the biblical story of Noah's flood and which I have linked to Plato's story. They wrote: "The Mediterranean was not a candidate. If the flood described in Genesis and Gilgamesh had been a real historic event, it would have to have been witnessed by modern humans—people with spoken language, the ability to plan ahead, an advanced cultural toolkit, but, most important, with a lifestyle endangered by the consequences of a flood. . . . So although the flooding of the Mediterranean from a Gibraltar waterfall was too ancient an event, it could still serve as a useful role model by suggesting which phenomena one would look for in the geological record for a much younger basin-filling catastrophe."[21]

Ryan and Pitman admit that the Gibraltar waterfall was the perfect candidate for a catastrophic flood that filled a giant basin. But their later research was primarily focused on the story of Noah's flood and its connection to the older *Gilgamesh Epic*, and there is little mention of Atlantis in their book. For our purposes, however, the discovery of the Mediterranean desiccation and the destruction of the Gibraltar dam provides an indispensable blueprint for the destruction that overcame Atlantis. Hsu seemed to entertain the idea more than once, at one point alluding to the connection between his discovery and the writings of H.G. Wells regarding the Mediterranean flood: "We had enough facts to formulate a working hypothesis, but what we did not realize was that our findings were to explain many long-standing puzzles that H.G. Wells had referred to as 'lost secrets of the Mediterranean' in one of his science fictions."[22]

Interestingly, H.G. Wells not only wrote about the Mediterranean flood long before the scientific proof became available, but he also dated it to a much more recent era, which, according to him, occurred between 10,000 and 30,000 B.C. Of course, this is within the timeline of Atlantis's empire according to Plato and Solon, who had taken great care to perpetuate what the Egyptian priests imparted as true history. In *The Outline of History* (1921), Wells wrote a chilling account of a Mediterranean flooding that could easily describe the experience of the Cretans and Atlanteans:

> Now, this may seem all the wildest speculation, but it is not entirely so, for if we examine a submarine contour map of the Straits of Gibraltar, we find there is an enormous valley running up from the Mediterranean deep, right through the Straits, and trenching some distance out on to the Atlantic shelf....This refilling of the Mediterranean, which by the rough chronology we are employing in this book may have happened somewhere between 30,000 and 10,000 B.C., must have been one of the greatest single events in the prehistory of our race. . . . Suddenly the ocean waters began to break through over the westward hills and to pour in upon these primitive peoples—the lake that had been their home and friend became their enemy; its waters rose and never abated; their settlements were submerged; the waters pursued them in their flight. Day by day and year by year the waters spread up the valleys and drove mankind before them. Many must have been surrounded and caught by the continually rising salt flood. It knew no check; it came faster and faster; it rose over the tree-tops, over the

hills, until it had filled the whole basin of the present Mediterranean and until it lapped the mountain cliffs of Arabia and Africa. Far away, long before the dawn of history, this catastrophe occurred.[23]

Figure 6:4
The Deluge, by Gustav Dore.

In light of all these facts and speculations, I believe that there is sufficient scientific information available to advance the hypothesis that Plato's description of the great deluge could well have occurred in the Mediterranean during the times of Atlantis.

Science necessarily moves slowly, and I am proposing a model that has previously been the province of speculation. The lapse of time that occurs between an initial scientific hypothesis, its examination and testing within the community, and its official acceptance can be decades long. For example, Dr. Hsu recounted the fact that with all the irrefutable evidence he and Bill Ryan had amassed during the expedition and even after the later corroborative data from their colleagues began pouring in, many scientists remained incredulous.

At the moment, scientists do not have the technological capability to definitively date all of the highly complex geological activities of a seismically active area, especially one as active as the Mediterranean. While we can date the period in which the Mediterranean completely dried up, leaving behind its telltale deposits, we cannot be sure of the number of times the Gibraltar dam has opened and closed its gates. It is quite likely that shorter cycles of partial evaporation and filling have taken place, leaving behind no detectable evidence of deposits. So, if the Mediterranean Sea had *begun* the process of evaporation but had not yet left salt deposits on the seafloor when the dam turned into a strait, then what signs can we look for to date the subsequent flood? The best we can say is this: Science has proven that the Mediterranean has gone through incessant climatic and geological changes. More importantly, examination of the seabed indicates that there have been numerous periods of dry, desert-like ages followed by torrential floods that had raised the coastline by as much as a mile.

No one can claim to know exactly how many times the Mediterranean Basin has been flooded, when each of these floods occurred, or the circumstances surrounding every multifaceted cataclysm. When it comes to summarizing the details of these newly discovered facts about the Mediterranean, even the summary of this subject in the *Encyclopaedia Britannica* leaves ample room for doubt: "Considerable uncertainty has remained regarding the chronology and character of sea–bottom salt formation, and evidence from subsequent seismic studies and core sampling has been subject to intense scientific debate."[24] Considering the fact that the discovery of the Mediterranean desiccation came only a few decades ago and that further expeditions have been rare, we are still at a guessing stage in our assessment of the chronology of many Mediterranean events.

For *our* purposes, however, enough scientific leads are available to suggest a working theory about the Mediterranean connection to Atlantis: Again, the earthquakes, volcanic eruptions, and basin-filling floods surrounding the demise of Atlantis are all there just as Plato described them. The date of the cataclysm could have been 10,000–30,000 B.C., as H.G. Wells theorized. These dates do coincide with the supposed reign of the Atlantean race according to Plato. After all, as H.S. Bellamy has pointed out, how could ancient geographers have known about the destruction of the Gibraltar dam if it occurred over five million years ago? So while we cannot definitively prove or disprove the theory based on scientific evidence alone, we certainly have a working hypothesis that can easily be correlated with the many other clues presented in this book.

Ranging from textual accounts to scientifically acquired information, enough material has been presented in this chapter to clearly show a connection between Atlantis and the eastern Mediterranean Sea. We have reviewed the literature from scientists and Atlantologists and have concluded that Atlantis, if it did indeed exist, was most likely situated in the Mediterranean. Having come this far, we are now ready to test the Mediterranean hypothesis and the case for Cyprus with the aid of technology unavailable to earlier generations of researchers. With the data from sonar mapping, and corresponding 3D models produced especially for this book, we can display accurate representations of seabed formations. We have targeted one such formation close to the island of Cyprus and will offer it for consideration. For those of us on the project, this location is an object of intense interest—one having the potential to solve the Atlantis mystery and, as a consequence, revolutionize our understanding of human prehistory.

7

Navel of the Earth

*Who dares claim that the archaeologists have
dug up all possible cultural vestiges?*

— C.W. Ceram
Gods, Graves, and Scholars (1949)

In previous chapters we have examined the origin, legacy, and modern impact of the Atlantis legend. We have seen how the notion of an extremely ancient and enigmatic civilization has captivated the imagination of people throughout history, and how the Atlantis theme reappears in worldwide myths, architectural motifs, literature, and sacred scriptures. We have also sifted through Plato's physical clues about Atlantis and have considered theories of its possible location, including the case for the Mediterranean and for the reality of the great cataclysm that Plato described.

Having come this far, we are now ready to locate the literal site, the actual remnants of Atlantis. Our case produces a treasure map of sorts, complete with a veritable *X* marking the spot—providing evidence for what would appear to be the archeological epicenter of Atlantis. We will shine new light on that mountainous island of legend that has cast a long shadow across the theater of human history.

All of the clues assembled in our search for Atlantis have drawn us steadily toward the eastern part of the Mediterranean Sea. In the present chapter, our attention will be focused on a more specific area within that geographic region, namely, the island of Cyprus and its environs. I believe that a striking case can be made for locating the remains of Atlantis on the sunken landmass just south of Cyprus.

Although the storyline of this "garden of the gods" forms the foundation for many of the most significant myths and legends worldwide, Plato's version of the story is decidedly more compelling because of the richness of its descriptive detail. The older, more generic legends allude to a land of utopian bliss populated by demigods; by contrast, Plato provides a uniquely thorough examination of the city plan that served as the capital of an empire. Over and above anything else, the *Critias* abounds with names, dates, measurements, and all sorts of factual information about the flora, fauna, agricultural produce, precious metals, and natural resources of a place he calls Atlantis.

Consider this account in the *Critias* of the way that the Atlanteans protected their main temples and palaces atop the Acropolis Hill by surrounding them with three concentric canals (or rings):

> They began by digging a canal three hundred feet wide, a hundred feet deep and fifty stades long from the sea to the outermost ring, thus making it accessible from the sea like a harbour; and they made the entrance to it large enough to admit the largest ships. At the bridges they made channels through the rings of land which separated those of water, large enough to admit the passage of a single trireme, and roofed over to make an underground tunnel; for the rims of the rings were of some height above the sea-level. The largest of the rings, to which there was access from the sea, was three stades in breadth and the ring of land within it the same. Of the second pair of the rings of water was two stades in breadth, and the ring of land again equal to it, while the ring of water running immediately round the central island was a stade across. The diameter of the island on which the palace was situated was five stades. It and the rings and the bridges (which were a hundred feet broad)

were enclosed by a stone wall all around, with towers and gates guarding the bridges on either side where they crossed the water. . . .[1]

This description is quite precise, perhaps even demanding by some standards. While it does not have the detail of a technical drawing, there is certainly enough information to enable the composition of blueprints.

Why would Plato bother with such superfluous information? Certainly, slogging through detail after detail in this manner would hardly be necessary for summoning forth one of Plato's hallmark allegories—although many Plato scholars hold fast to this theory. Other skeptics believe that Plato must have drifted off into some sort of ancient Greek version of a science-fiction fantasy. Still other commentators point to the fact that the dialog ends abruptly in midsentence as evidence that Plato must have abandoned the story as unworthy of further development. But all such literary speculations still beg the question: What happens if we simply take Plato's word at face value? This book shows the startling result.

Figure 7:1
Satellite image of the eastern Mediterranean Sea, the possible location of the island of Atlantis.

The crucial point for our investigation turns out to be the general credibility of Plato himself. If the Atlantis myth had been propagated by some ancient, unknown storyteller, it is doubtful that the tale would still be receiving attention. However, the author of this legend was a prime architect of Western thought—a towering genius about whom Alfred North Whitehead famously remarked that all philosophy for the last two millennia amounted to no more than mere "footnotes to Plato"!

No doubt, my respect for Plato was among the reasons I found myself obsessed with the mission of finding Atlantis. Perhaps it was also because of my incurable fascination with ancient mythology, history, and architecture that a project of constructing a map of the Mediterranean seafloor began in earnest. But in time it became apparent that my only hope of solving the Atlantis riddle was to look for hard evidence in a specific location, using suitable means.

Island of Love

Oh! To make my way to Cyprus, isle of Aphrodite,
where dwell the love-gods strong to soothe man's soul, or to Paphos,
which that foreign river, never fed by rain, enriches with its hundred mouths!
Oh! Lead me, Bromian god, celestial guide of Bacchic pilgrims,
to the hallowed slopes of Olympus, where Pierian Muses have
their haunt most fair. There dwell the Graces; there is soft desire;
there thy votaries may hold their revels freely.

— Euripides
The Bacchantes (410 B.C.)

Aside from the previous analysis of possible Near East locations, my focus was drawn to the easternmost part of the Mediterranean Basin for several reasons. Most importantly, after reviewing the general bathymetric maps of the Mediterranean, it became obvious that the

Atlantis Plato described could only exist in a few isolated spots. Specific references to a smooth and rectangular plain surrounded by mountains, facing south, and sheltered from cold winds by lofty mountains to the north, left little ambiguity. As outlined in chapter 3, Plato's clues about the mountainous island of Atlantis and the rectangular plain at its foothills also reveal that the whole landmass stretched in an east/west direction.

After examining the few crude bathymetric maps that were available in the public domain, it was clear to me that the real estate on the seafloor of the eastern Mediterranean had potential, and even more intriguing was the fact that very little was known about the area. According to a leading expert on the eastern Mediterranean seafloor, Dr. John K. Hall, "the eastern Mediterranean has historically been the most poorly mapped part of the Mediterranean. The reasons for this have been political, geographical, and sociological. . . . there has been renewed interest in this sediment-filled end of the Mediterranean whose genesis, age, and geological and tectonic framework continue to invite, incite, or excite much speculation."[2]

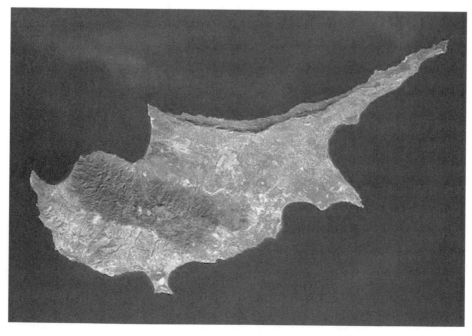

Figure 7:2
Island of Cyprus. (satellite image)

Aside from geology, there were many reasons to focus on the general vicinity of Cyprus. I have shown that historical and mythological factors provided valuable indicators. For example, Poseidon is clearly associated with Atlantis in Plato's account, but I was soon to discover that the symbol of the three-pronged trident carried by Poseidon may actually represent the Atlantean empire. According to Ignatius Donnelly the trident was "an emblem of the three continents that were embraced in the empire of Atlantis."[3] Indeed, Cyprus is famous for its location at the crossroads of three continents: Europe, Asia, and Africa. Its strategic position in the eastern Mediterranean has rendered this small island an important outpost for a long series of dominant political powers that have come and gone over the centuries.

Perhaps more important, Cyprus is located near the epicenter of various myths about the "Garden." The eastern Mediterranean is home to almost everything related to the mystery gods of ancient times. Cult centers of the gods who had supposedly descended from the heavens with the gift of civilization can be found in Egypt, Greece, Rome, Turkey, Mesopotamia, Persia, Palestine, and Cyprus itself. We have noted that diluted forms of what I have called the universal myth are found throughout the world, but there is little doubt that the greatest concentration of tales and legends emanated from areas that literally surround the island of Cyprus. It is perfectly nestled in the heart of the area known as the cradle of human culture.

Cyprus is also the legendary birthplace of Aphrodite and Adonis; it is richly connected to the Olympian gods of Greek mythology. Aphrodite (or Venus to the Romans) was said to be born from the foam of the sea at the southern shores of Cyprus and received by the "assembly of the gods." This endearing story of the Greek goddess of love and beauty has been an endless source of inspiration for artists throughout the ages. Aphrodite's famous temple at Paphos on the island of Cyprus—where she reportedly first appeared—was a major pilgrimage destination for devotees of

Figure 7:3
Aphrodite rising from the sea
by the shores of Cyprus.
(painting by Freydoon Rassouli)

the goddess. Her worshippers believed that immediately after her appearance, "wherever her feet touched the ground there blossomed all manner of flowering plants. The Graces then dressed her in the kind of attire that they themselves assumed when attending the dances of the immortals, decking her in a crown of gold, luxurious gowns and jewels including a magic girdle—the famous *kestos imas*. Accompanied by Eros and Pathos, the god of longing, she journeyed thence to Olympus in order to claim her place among the assembly of the gods."[4]

More important for us is the striking resemblance between Aphrodite's home and Plato's description of Atlantis. Plato wrote that the main temples of Atlantis City were situated at the summit of the Acropolis Hill, a holy area that was encircled by a golden wall glistening with precious metals and jewels, and it was difficult to reach. He also said that two springs rushed out from the central headquarters of Atlantis, one with hot water and the other cold, and that the whole area was incredibly lush and fertile. Compare this with a typical description of Aphrodite's home: According to the Cypriot mythologist Stass Paraskos, her estate was "surrounded by a golden fence, containing palaces of gold and precious stones. This was situated on a mountain of Cyprus, inaccessible to mortals, where a sweet climate prevailed, where the soil produces without being cultivated, and where there are two springs among green foliage. There lived Aphrodite surrounded by Erotes: a kind of

Paradise which has been identified with the site known as the Baths of Aphrodite."[5]

Allusions to the Atlantis legend survive even today in Cypriot folklore. Every year, during the first days of June, the people of Cyprus celebrate a colorful holiday called the Kataklysmos, otherwise known as the Festival of the Flood. The feast is so ancient that no one knows when the practice began. However, it is known to predate Christianity and probably originated with native myths surrounding Aphrodite and Adonis. After its assimilation into Christianity, the festival took on new and very different religious connotations, coinciding now with the Day of Pentecost. The three-day holiday is initiated by a solemn procession, with a priest carrying the Precious Cross to the seaside where, after prayers, it is thrown into the Mediterranean Sea. The most popular feature of the festivities is the practice of throwing water on one another, symbolizing the purification of the body as well as the soul. Could it be that this harkens to the distant memory of the great flood, when humanity was supposedly purged of its sins and purified through expiation by water? This Festival of the Flood, or Kataklysmos—a name derived from the etymological source for the word *cataclysm*—is unique to Cyprus, an island that, according to our interpretation, suffered the greatest cataclysm of flooding of all time!

All of these clues seemed to provide circumstantial evidence for the Levantine Basin as a possible location for Atlantis, especially in that area lying between Cyprus and Syria. However, in order to support our circumstantial evidence with real visual data, a look at the actual seafloor was necessary. At the time, maps showing the underwater topography of the eastern Mediterranean lacked sufficient detail to make any kind of positive correlation with features supplied in Plato's account of Atlantis.

Obviously, detailed bathymetric maps would incontrovertibly prove or else purge the Cyprus theory. Thus began the search for more hard data.

NOAA's Ark

*Humans have scrutinized perhaps a millionth or a billionth
of the sea's darkness. Maybe less. Maybe much less.*

— William Broad
The Universe Below: Discovering
the Secrets of the Deep Sea (1997)

It is understandable that the Mediterranean should tantalize treasure
hunters. In a world whose land surfaces have been thoroughly
explored and mapped, the submerged seafloors of earth remain
irresistible to adventurers who know that it hides many secrets. The
remarkable explosion of technological progress in the twentieth
century has finally allowed them to peek under the world's oceans,
seas, and lakes.For the moment, however, the marine scientists I
spoke to at the National Geophysical Data Center told me that we
know more about the surface of Mars than about the topography
of our own seafloors.While visiting this center, which is part of the
National Oceanic and Atmospheric Association (NOAA) complex
in Boulder, Colorado, I was briefed on the techniques for gathering
data from the seafloor. Since radar does not penetrate water, the
only way of acquiring detailed data is through specially designed
sonar devices, which are attached to cables and dragged through the
water behind research vessels as they slowly zigzag across a prede-
fined survey area—a very expensive and time-consuming process.[6]

Although the master databases at NOAA did not have detailed
information about the eastern Mediterranean, they did have access
to a new set of data published by Dr. John K. Hall. The data had
been acquired by two separate cruises in 1987 and 1990, but had
not yet been incorporated into NOAA's master database. At the
time it seemed like a miracle to finally possess such vital and hard-
to-find data.

The relatively large amount of digital data concerned with
the Cyprus area had been obtained through soundings conducted
aboard the *R/V Akademik Nikolaj Starkhov,* a 75-meter vessel spon-
sored by the Geological Institute of the Russian Academy of

Sciences. This research ship was outfitted for modern geophysical, stratigraphic, and lithological investigations. According to Dr. Hall, in a published a report on the project, "the aim of the voyage was to examine the geological structure of the eastern Mediterranean between Syria and Cyprus, south and west of the island, and to compare the land structures in southern Cyprus with those in northwestern Syria."[7]

The expedition included international experts in various fields, including oceanography, meteorology, marine biology, remote sensing, and modeling. The raw data gathered was further processed by scientists from various organizations in Germany, Russia, and Israel. Although the cartography and bathymetry of the Mediterranean were of great interest—even to ancient sailors—this was among the

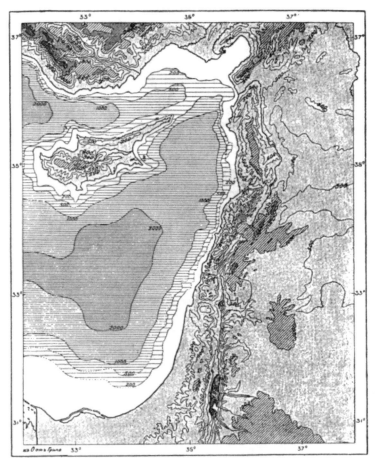

Figure 7:4
Bathymetric map of the eastern Mediterranean,
late 19th century.

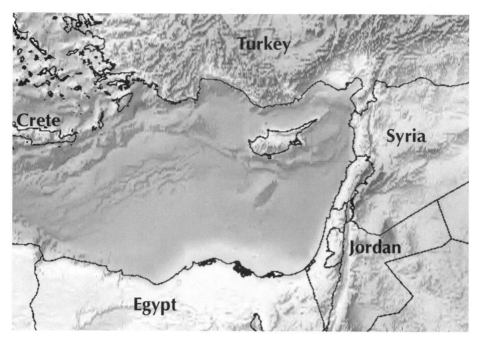

Figure 7:5
NOAA's map of the eastern Mediterranean seafloor.

first occasions in history that the details of the eastern Mediterranean would be examined and mapped, and the very first time that it would be accomplished through the use of multibeam sonar, a vastly superior technology compared to the previous single-beam instruments.[8]

Figure 7:6
Research vessel *Akademik Nikolaj Strakhov* of the Geological Institute of the Russian Academy of Sciences, Moscow.

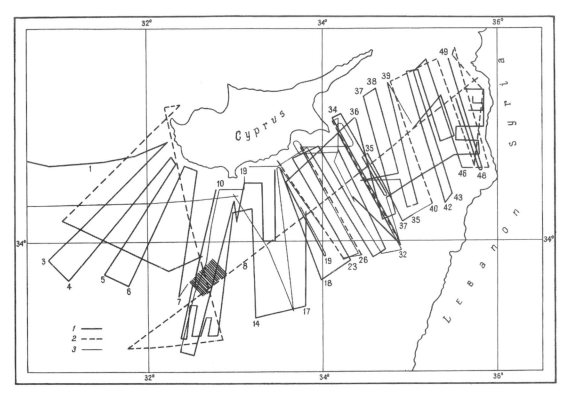

Figure 7:7
Geophysical investigations during Cruise 5 of the *R/V Akademik Nikolaj Strakhov*.
Zigzag lines show the path of the vessel while gathering bathymetric data.

While Dr. Hall did produce and publish his own bathymetric maps and 3D models from the digital data gathered during the expedition, they were unfortunately not detailed enough for my purpose of authenticating or matching the landscape with Plato's description of Atlantis. Thus began a personal project to produce meticulous and accurate bathymetric maps of the so-called Cyprus Arc and the Levantine Basin, using the same data that had been obtained by the Russian vessels but now deploying state-of-the-art American rendering technology. This chance meeting at NOAA and the later acquisition of the digital data proved to be crucial to a map-making process that took more than two years to complete.

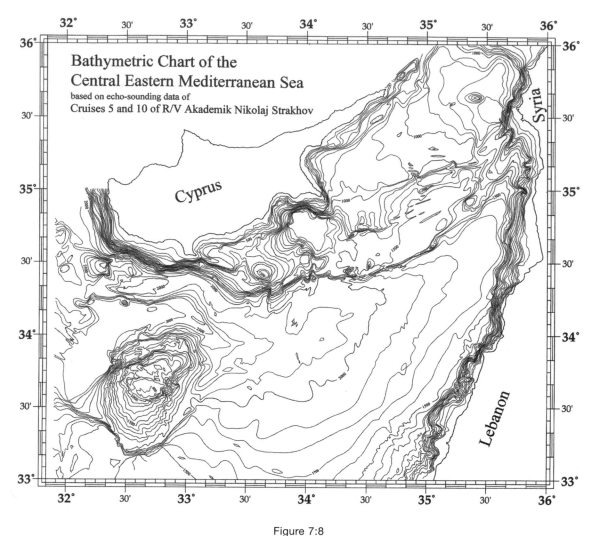

Figure 7:8
Dr. Hall's map of the northeastern Mediterranean seafloor.

This more advanced mapmaking project was funded by Michael Wisenbaker, president of Heritage Standard Corporation in Dallas, Texas. His company drills for deep gas in the Delaware Basin of west Texas and New Mexico. The gas is often found at depths in excess of 20,000 feet, discovered with the help of imaging technology that displays reservoir and petrophysical data in 3D. The ability to image at these depths was essential for creating our maps. Mr. Wisenbaker also introduced me to his own contractor for this work, the Scotia Group, Inc., an oil and gas advisory service company that employs image-enhancing software to model different exploration targets throughout the world.[9]

Using the bathymetric data obtained at NOAA, the Scotia Group produced enhanced seafloor maps of our target area near Cyprus. In conjunction with this effort, they produced a 3D computer model of the topography that allowed interactive manipulations of the image. When simulated motion is added, one is enabled to "fly" around the landscape and view landform details from different angles. Next, the shoreline and elevation data were superimposed, giving a view of the whole eastern Mediterranean area, above and below the water. Finally, through the creative work of Patrick Lowry, a senior vice president at the Scotia Group, special programs were created to accurately depict and animate the flooding and drying up of the Mediterranean at various depths.

Remarkably, my own modest Atlantis research has resulted in the production of the world's first high-resolution maps of the eastern Mediterranean, an unexpected side benefit that may be of use for other scientific or commercial efforts in the region. What began as simple curiosity about whether Atlantis might lay hidden in the eastern Mediterranean had, for the moment, turned into full-time work in cartography!

Our 3D maps were produced between the years 2000 and 2002 and are being published here for the first time.[10] The aim is to demonstrate the points of correspondence between the present-day topography of the seafloor and the identifying marks of Atlantis compiled in chapter 3.[11] Readers are encouraged to scrutinize these images and reach their own conclusions based on the evidence. We, however, believe there is a match—that the points of correspondence are not coincidental, and that there are good reasons to suggest we in fact have our *X* that marks the spot.

Discovery of Atlantis

And from your happy island while I sail,
let Cyprus send for me a favoring gale;
may she advance, and bless your new command,
prosper your town, and send me safe to land.

— **Solon**
Plutarch's Lives (75 A.D.)

As we discovered in chapter 6, the Mediterranean Sea has been subject to immense geological changes during its long and turbulent history. We learned that the Mediterranean was at one time a desert spotted with lakes and lagoons, and this scientific fact led us

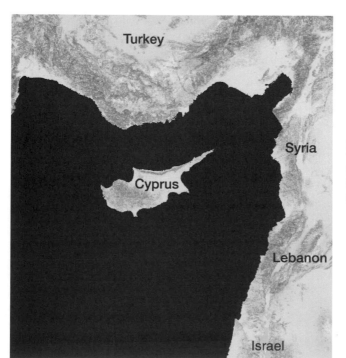

Figure 8:1
The eastern
Mediterranean
Sea at present
sea level.

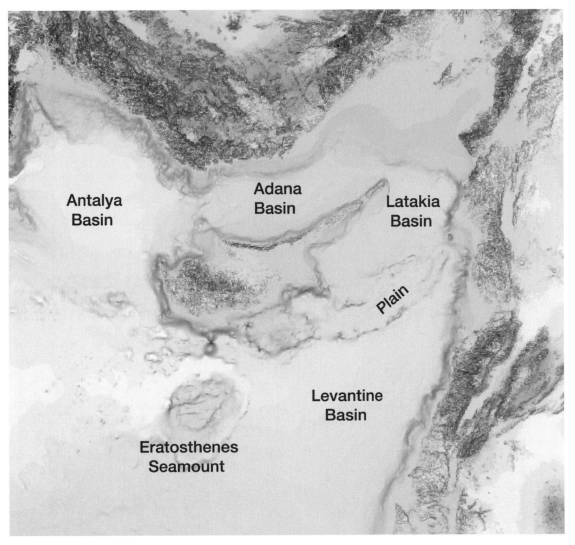

Figure 8:2
The eastern Mediterranean Basin.

to conclude that Atlantis may have sunk to its depths in the wake of the greatest deluge of human history. In line with this theory, Figure 8:1 depicts the eastern Mediterranean Basin as it appears today, filled with water; Figure 8:2 shows the basin much as it would have appeared at a point of maximum evaporation, when it was a vast desert.

Figures 8:3 through 8:5 clearly show a long and rectangular submarine valley to the southeast of Cyprus, stretching toward the coast of Syria. It faces south and is sheltered from the north by the long arm of Cyprus, known to locals as the "panhandle." It also stretches in an east/west direction just as Plato described.

As I noted in the last chapter, computer graphics technology has been crucial in this research. Using special software developed for our project by the Scotia Group, we were able to depict the Mediterranean Basin at different fill levels during its geologic history. This in turn permitted us to represent coastline and underwater formations as they may have appeared at various stages during an evaporative cycle. In particular, in order to see how Atlantis Island might have manifested itself at some point along the water level continuum, we studied the appearance of the basin at various sea levels.

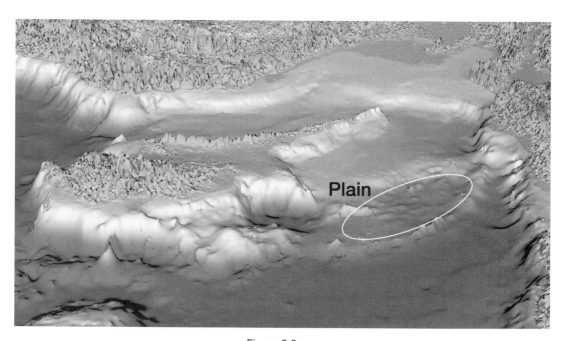

Figure 8:3
A rectangular plain [within the oval] that stretches in an east/west direction,
as Plato described, appears underwater off the Cyprus coast.

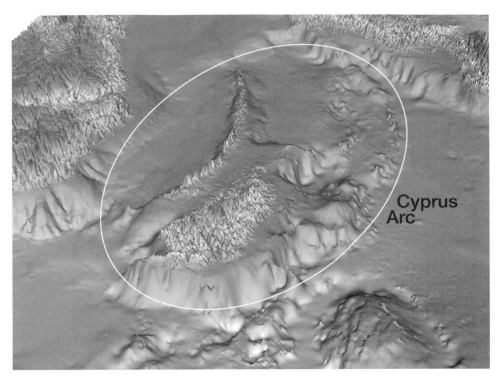

Figure 8:4
The eastern Mediterranean Basin and the Cyprus Arc. (viewed from the west)

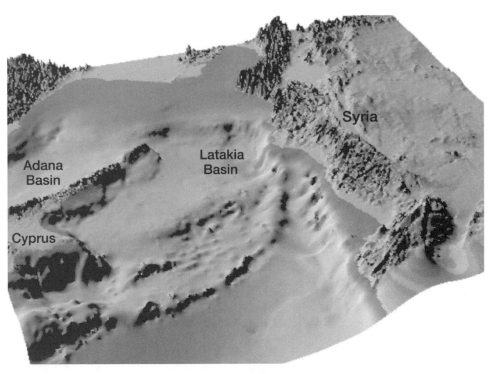

Figure 8:5
The long and rectangular plain of Atlantis, resting between Cyprus and Syria.

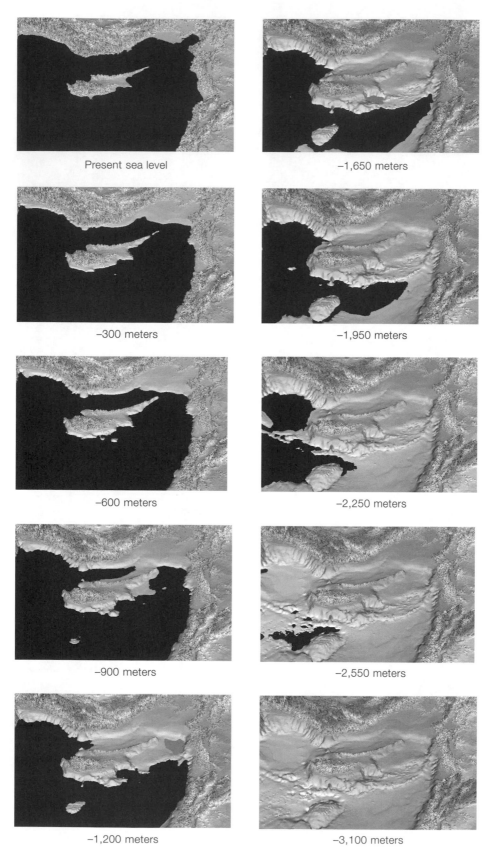

Present sea level

−300 meters

−600 meters

−900 meters

−1,200 meters

−1,650 meters

−1,950 meters

−2,250 meters

−2,550 meters

−3,100 meters

Figure 8:6
The emptying of the Mediterranean Sea in 300-meter intervals.

As can be seen in Figure 8.6, the software allowed us to accurately animate the cycle of emptying and flooding in the easternmost part of the Mediterranean. There is little doubt that this work has resulted in the most detailed and realistic computer visualization of the great Mediterranean "salinity crisis" to date, including the inundation of Cyprus by Atlantic waters.

Simulating the progressively shrinking water levels in our computer model led to this result: When 1,650 meters of water had been subtracted from current sea levels, the Cyprus Arc was raised completely above water. The consequences of this discovery were both exhilarating and puzzling. The exhilaration was immediate in that the Plain of Atlantis seemed to materialize before our eyes. But a problem remained: By "draining" the Mediterranean to the levels

Figure 8:7
The eastern Mediterranean area as it would have appeared when the sea's depth was 1,650 meters (more than one mile) below today's level.

Figure 8:8
Northeasterly view of the eastern Mediterranean as it would have appeared
when the sea's depth was 1,650 meters below today's level.

at which the Plain of Atlantis would have been an elevated surface, we also produced the rather unwelcome effect of rendering so much of the Cyprus Arc above water that our hypothesized Atlantis appeared as neither an island nor a true peninsula (see Figures 8:7 and 8:8).

What we had failed to account for in our computer simulation, we discovered, were the regional sources of water input from rivers originating in the Turkish and Cyprus highlands. The mountains which surround the area between Cyprus and Turkey generate large amounts of precipitation that collect into extensive river systems and empty into the northeastern Mediterranean (Figure 8:9).

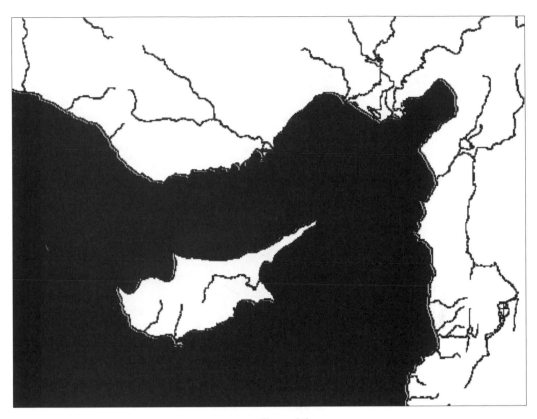

Figure 8:9
Major rivers of the northeastern Mediterranean region today.
(NOAA map)

Judging by current hydrologic processes, we believe it safe to assume that nearly all of the rivers that presently empty into the northeasternmost Mediterranean Sea would have behaved similarly in the days of Atlantis. They would have collected in the Latakia Basin near the eastern coast of today's Cyprus. The rivers that flow down the Taurus range in southeastern Turkey, along with those flowing from the Kyrenia mountain range of northern Cyprus, would have pooled in the Adana and Cilicia Basins, which together run the length of Cyprus Island parallel to the coast of Turkey.[1] When estimations of these river paths were added to the simulation software, the effect was to render an illustration of the Cyprus Arc

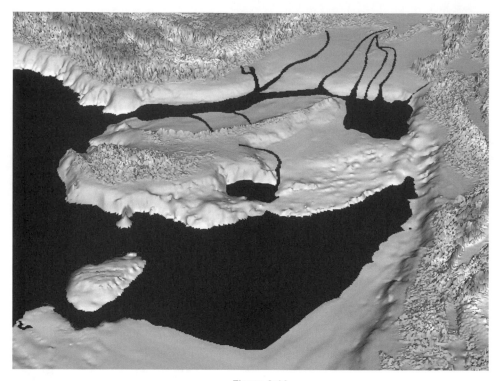

Figure 8:10
Rivers extended to the antediluvian valleys.

showing the basins and troughs filled with water. This produced an image of a distinct peninsula that projected westward from the present-day coast of Syria—there connected by a narrow neck composed largely of the formation known as the West Tartus Ridge (Figure 8:10).

It should be kept in mind that while there is some degree of uncertainty in the construction of these models, they are nonetheless based on real, quantifiable data. The lowering of the Mediterranean water levels by 1,650 meters and the subsequent addition of river paths and fresh water input produced a striking image of a large island or peninsula.

We can also demonstrate that our modeling of Atlantis Island corresponds not only to clues extracted from Plato, but to well-known illustrations of Atlantis. A simple visual comparison between the best-known drawing of Atlantis from Plato's description and our sonar-based recreation of antediluvian Cyprus offers an eerie similarity (Figures 8:11 and 8:12).

136

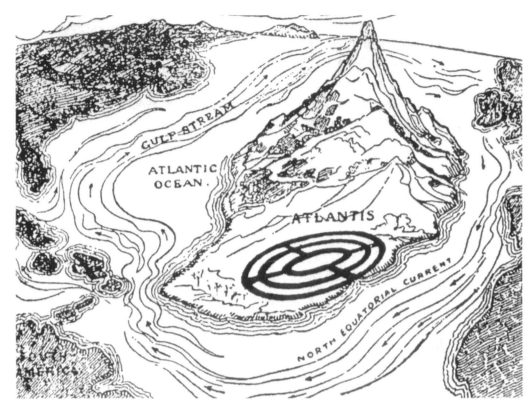

Figure 8:11
Atlantis according to Plato's description.

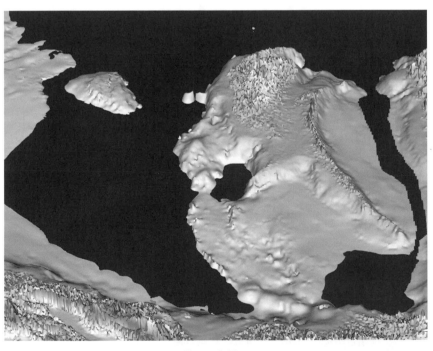

Figure 8:12
Cyprus in its antediluvian state, as viewed from the east, resembles the well-known artist's
conception of Atlantis shown in Figure 8:11 above. Note especially the plain area in each.

View of Atlantis Island

Ye Gods, from whom these miracles did spring,
inspire my numbers with celestial heat. . . .

— Ovid
Metamorphoses (1 A.D.)

Was this really Atlantis? It all seemed quite incredible. All of us on the project were experiencing a "Eureka!" phenomenon, but at the same time we worried that some critical detail may have been missed or a faulty assumption might have crept into in our methodology. I went back and carefully reviewed our work—and then I realized and fully accepted that I must stand behind what is here being presented to the world.

In what follows, then, I will attempt to pull all of our findings together by comparing our empirical maps and models of the eastern Mediterranean seafloor with all of the inferences that can be reasonably made from Plato's description. I believe that this point-by-point correlation of the evidence linking Atlantis to Cyprus cannot be coincidental.

For the sake of clarity we will classify the list of identifying marks that were compiled earlier in chapter 3 into four distinct categories:

- The description of the whole island of Atlantis.
- The description of the great rectangular Plain of Atlantis.
- The description of the capital city of Atlantis.
- The description of Atlantis's flora and fauna, its wildlife, and the island's natural resources.

We will begin by considering Plato's portrayal of the island itself, which we showed earlier was one of the primary sets of clues in the *Critias:*

> To begin with the region as a whole was said to be high above the level of the sea, from which it rose precipitously. . . .

Atlantis Island rose sharply from the sea and its mountains were considerably elevated. This point matches our recreation of the antediluvian state of Cyprus as shown in Figure 8:3. The island's foundation rises almost vertically from the seafloor for nearly a mile before reaching the present coastline of Cyprus. From there, the Troodos Massif, Cyprus's highest mountain range, rises for another 1.2 miles before peaking at Mount Olympus. In other words, the highest point of the island in its antediluvian form would have been over 2 miles above sea level. Our island would have towered prominently above the sea, "from which it rose precipitously."

We also know from Plato's account that Atlantis was close to several nearby islands that once served as stepping-stones to other continents. Cyprus is currently the third largest island in the

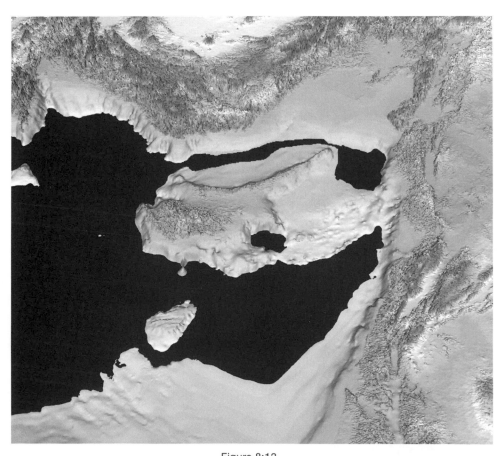

Figure 8:13
Plato indicated that Atlantis was once adjacent to "stepping-stone" islands.
At antediluvian water levels, several islands emerge in to view southwest of Cyprus.

Mediterranean, but it was much larger in its antediluvian state—about twice its present size. The nearby islands today are Rhodes and Crete; however, by lowering the sea level, a number of currently submerged structures emerge as islands, more in line with Plato's description of other islands as "stepping-stones." Figure 8:13 indeed shows "other islands" to the south and west of Cyprus that might have served as a passageway to the continents of Africa and Europe respectively.

The largest of these is the Eratosthenes Seamount, just a few miles south of Cyprus. This landform was first discovered in the 1960s and is considered to be "one of the remarkable bottom structures of the eastern Mediterranean Sea."[2] The Russian research vessel *(R/V Akademik Nikolaj Strakhov,* Cruise 5*)* that gathered the bathymetric data used in the creation of our models conducted extensive surveys on the seamount. The core samples taken from its flattopped summit were examined and indicated that its summit was at one time dry land that, not surprisingly, had been subjected to recurrent inundations.[3]

What, then, in review, could explain Plato's reference to the actual sinking of Atlantis? The Levantine Basin forms the "basic bottom"'of the eastern Mediterranean seafloor. It has been our inference that the sheer weight of the massive body of water that filled the basin, during a process that according to scientists took over one hundred years, may have forced the Levantine Basin to sink. In other words, the Atlantis portion of the Cyprus Arc would have been submerged through the combined effect of rising waters as well as the sinking of the basin on which it stood—a submergence in line with that reported in the *Critias,* again pointing to Cyprus and the eastern Mediterranean as the correct location.

As we have clearly seen, Cyprus also matches the description of Atlantis's susceptibility to floods, earthquakes, and volcanoes. In fact, it is positioned within a territory that is subject to some of the most violent natural disasters known to have occurred in the history of our planet.

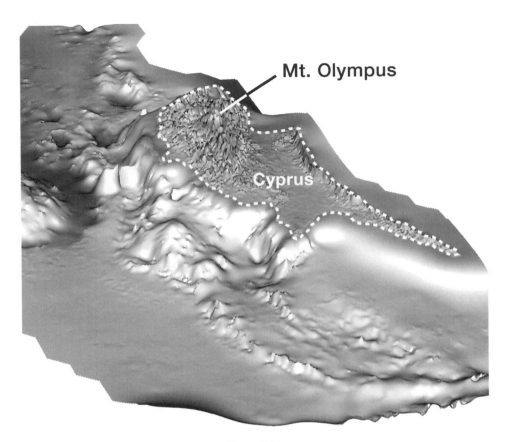

Mt. Olympus

Cyprus

Figure 8:14
Cyprus was created by the collision of tectonic plates, making the
island one of the most famous ophiolite bodies in the world.

Another salient fact is the geographic location of the island:
Situated north of Egypt and east of Greece, Cyprus is just a few
hundred miles from the two lands that brought us the legend of
Atlantis.

Further, Plato's reference to the numerous hot springs on
Atlantis led us to conclude that the island must have been composed
of igneous rock. Cyprus has hot and cold springs and is of major
importance to geologists due to its incredible natural history.
Dr. Hall wrote, "The eastern Mediterranean is perhaps the most
important area for understanding one of the key events in the
history of the Earth. The closing of the Neo-Tethys at the end of
the Mesozoic formed huge nappes and ophiolite bodies. . . ."[4]

Ophiolites are sections of oceanic crust, pushed up to the earth's surface through tectonic forces, which form the igneous rocks that are often found along both convergent and divergent plate boundaries. The island of Cyprus was literally formed through the collision of tectonic plates. Its famous Troodos Massif is of great interest to geologists, who "have concluded that the range, made up of igneous rock, was formed from molten rock beneath the deep ocean (Tethys) that once separated the continents of Eurasia and Afro-Arabia."[5] This means that the very highest peak on the island, which is over two miles above its foundation, was once on the seafloor. Geology scholars have made Cyprus a favorite research destination for this very reason.

Other matches between Cyprus and Plato's specific references to Atlantis Island are as follows: Cyprus is neither very close nor very far from the equator and enjoys an idyllic location, as it is situated in a subtropical zone with mild, wet winters and hot, dry summers. The high peaks of Mt. Olympus do indeed collect snowfall, serving as popular sites for tourists during the ski season. In addition, there are marshes, swamps, numerous rivers, high mountains, and a rectangular plain at the southern base of the Cyprus Arc.

The major rivers of present-day Cyprus originate at the high peaks of Mt. Olympus and descend in every direction to the fertile valleys below. The abundant rainwater on the highlands of Cyprus drains through fractures and reemerges at low altitudes in the form of springs, or flows in streams to the lowlands where it replenishes local aquifers. These could once have been the rivers of Atlantis, which reportedly flowed from the surrounding highlands down to the rectangular valley below, nourishing the plain of Atlantis throughout the year. Plato wrote a detailed account, as we saw earlier, about how the Atlanteans collected the fresh water flowing from the northern mountains by means of a ditch dug around the great plain, which subsequently fed an immense network of irrigation channels within its borders.[6]

That said, it may be helpful to once again list the identifiers of Atlantis Island that I previously compiled, so that these can be studied alongside the images of the antediluvian form of Cyprus suggested in our computer model.

Details of Atlantis Island	Match with Cyprus
— Atlantis Island rose sharply from the sea.	√
— There were smaller islands nearby that served as stepping-stones to surrounding continents.	√
— The mountainous island rose to a very high level above the sea.	√
— The island was north of the equator.	√
— Atlantis had both a winter and a summer.	√
— Atlantis was neither very close nor very far from the equator.	√
— The plain was in a valley.	√
— There was snowfall on the highest peaks of Atlantis.	√
— The island's rivers originated on the highlands.	√
— The island was composed of igneous rock.	√
— Atlantis had hot springs and cold springs.	√
— Atlantis was located on or around an area that experienced volcanic activity.	√
— Atlantis was "swallowed up by the earth."	√
— Atlantis was prone to violent seismic activity and flooding.	√
— The Atlantean empire embraced three continents: Europe, Asia, and Africa.	√

View of the Great Plain of Atlantis

Olympus is the abode of the gods that stands fast forever.
Neither is it shaken by winds nor ever wet with rain,
nor does snow fall upon it, but the air is outspread clear
and cloudless, and over it hovers a radiant whiteness.
Therein the blessed gods are glad all their days. . . .

— Homer
Odyssey (800 B.C.)

We have illustrated points of comparison between the prehistoric state of the Cyprus Arc and Plato's description of Atlantis. But the *Critias* provides further clues concerning the great plain of the island, and so our spotlight now shifts from Atlantis Island as a whole to the flat, rectangular plain stretching along its southern foothills. What we discover in this case is stunning: In nearly every detail provided by Plato, our unique models of the rectangular submarine valley that extends from southeastern Cyprus to the Syrian shoreline correlate with his descriptions of the plain of Atlantis. Scientists have yet to name this submerged valley, but it is generally considered to be a part of the Cyprus Arc. I would suggest however, that it may already have a name—that being the great Plain of Atlantis!

As we know, Plato wrote that Atlantis City was "surrounded by a uniformly flat plain, which was in turn enclosed by mountains which came right down to the sea." We are also told that the plain was rectangular in shape and that "this whole area of the island faced south, and was sheltered from the north winds." And now, over two millennia later, Figure 8:15 reveals what can in fact be found here at the bottom of the eastern Mediterranean Sea: a uniformly flat and —just as Plato said—a "naturally long, regular rectangle" in the form of a submarine valley that stretches from Cyprus toward the coast of Syria. And this rectangle is indeed enclosed by mountains which would have descended "right down to the sea"; further, it even faces south, sheltered from the north by the northeastern arm of Cyprus (Karpas Peninsula).

144

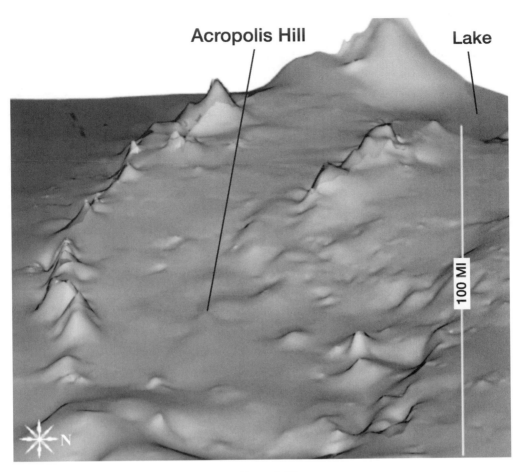

Acropolis Hill   **Lake**

100 MI

N

Figure 8:15
Close-up view of the rectangular plain of Atlantis.
(view towards northwest)

The great Plain of Atlantis is often depicted as surrounded by mountains on three sides, with the plain itself stretching along the southern foothills of the island. Plato wrote that "the mountains which surrounded it [the plain] were celebrated as being more numerous, higher and more beautiful than any which exist today."[7] We see similar depictions in early Greek mythology, where the island supposedly "lay spread out like a disk, with mountains rising from it, and the vault of heaven appearing to rest upon its outer edges all around."[8]

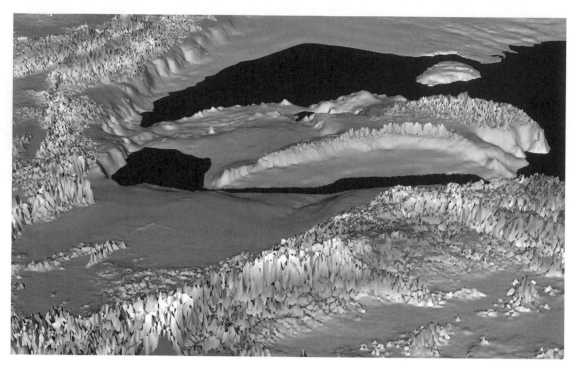

Figure 8:16
Atlantis viewed from the north, surrounded by mountains.

Figure 8:16 shows how the Plain of Atlantis was literally surrounded by mountains on every side, with a string of coastal hills protecting its southern border. Surprisingly, even this minute detail is corroborated by ancient Greek mythology. Ignatius Donnelly wrote that "Greek mythology, in speaking of the Garden of the Hesperides, tells us that 'the outer edge of the garden was slightly raised, so that the water might not run in and overflow the land'."[9] Viewed from the north, it shows the rectangular plain and indeed the whole island surrounded by an array of mountain ranges extending all the way from western Turkey to Syria, continuing southward to Lebanon and Israel.

We surmised earlier that since the island of Atlantis was supposed to house towering mountains that were mostly submerged after the flood, the rectangular plain at its southern foothills must now lie in deep waters. The Plain of Atlantis and its mountain ranges in our model are as much as one mile below today's water level. We also proposed that the smooth and flat plain must have been close to sea level since ships supposedly sailed directly from the plain's southern border to the Acropolis Hill, which was "near the middle of the plain." Moreover, careful scrutiny led us to conclude that since the rectangular plain faced south and was parallel to the "greatest length" of the island itself, both the island and its southern plain must have stretched in an east/west direction. As Plato indicated, all of these points match correctly.

The submerged plain is surrounded on three sides by towering mountains that would have formed a natural fortress prior to the inundation. Any ancient king would have coveted such a beautiful, fertile, and ideally located island. The rectangular plain is smooth, relatively flat, and would have been a prime location for building cities. The rivers "which flowed down the mountains" would have supplied abundant fresh water for the irrigation channels, creating a lush landscape, promoting agricultural production. Clouds would have gathered around the surrounding mountains and provided copious rainfall, leaving the southern valley in a rain shadow that would have seldom seen rain.

The only remaining clue from Plato's account of the rectangular plain deals with its size. As we saw in chapter 3, the *Critias* actually provides two contradictory bits of information about the length and width of the plain. On one hand we are specifically told that it was 330 miles long and 220 miles wide, while on the other hand we are told that the capital city of Atlantis was only seven miles from the southern sea, even though it was supposedly near its middle. Both of these details cannot simultaneously be true. Further study led us to conclude that the plain was likely much smaller than the 330/220 mile description and was probably about one tenth that size, since the alternative would render the whole island much too vast. And indeed, the submerged plain stretching between Cyprus and Syria is, coincidentally, about 33 miles long and 22 miles wide!

In this section we have successfully matched the antediluvian state of the Cyprus Arc with Plato's description of Atlantis Island. This section showed further similarities between the southeastern edge of the Cyprus Arc and the great Plain of Atlantis:

Details of the Great Plain of Atlantis	Match with Cyprus
— The plain was long and rectangular.	√
— Mountains that came right down to the sea surrounded the plain.	√
— The plain now rests in deep-sea levels.	√
— The plain was uniformly flat.	√
— The plain was very beautiful, fertile, and near the sea.	√
— The plain faced south.	√
— The plain was roughly 33 miles long and 22 miles wide.	√
— The island's northern mountains sheltered the plain from cold northerly winds.	√
— The mountains that surrounded Atlantis proper were "numerous, higher, and more beautiful than any which exist today."	√
— Both the island and its southern plain were long and rectangular.	√
— They ran parallel with one another in an east/west direction.	√
— The plain was in a valley.	√
— The Plain of Atlantis was close to sea level.	√

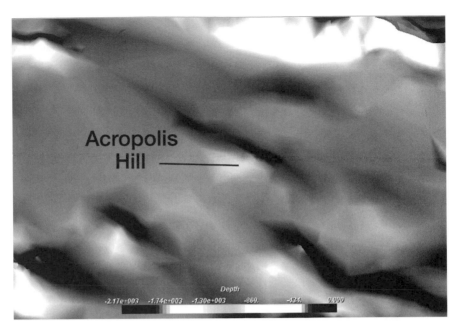

Figure 8:17
The Acropolis Hill "near the middle" of the great Plain of Atlantis.

View of Atlantis City

*What a light shot through my mind! Atlantis! The Atlantis
of Plato, that continent denied by Origen and Humbolt, who
placed its disappearance amongst the legendary tales.
I had it there now before my eyes, bearing upon it the
unexceptionable testimony of its catastrophe.*

— Jules Verne
20,000 Leagues under the Sea (1869)

Near the middle of the rectangular plain at the foothills of the
island, and only a few miles away from the southern sea, Atlantis
City once shone as the most beautiful spot on earth. Its bejeweled
temples and metallic walls glistened under the tropical sun, visible
for miles. And Atlantis, had it survived, would no doubt have
dwarfed all the wonders of the ancient world to follow. The city
planners had effectively combined sophisticated architectural styles
with lush gardens, ingenious landscaping, and exquisite artwork.

One can almost feel Plato's awe and wonderment as he narrates the story of the splendor of the city in his recounting of Solon's words.[10]

But was it real? Many believe so, and our research seems to increasingly corroborate the authenticity of our own hypothesis.

During earlier phases of the project, while the outlines of Atlantis Island were emerging on our computer model, we were excited, but we were little prepared for the heady emotions that would accompany the discovery of what may very well be Acropolis Hill itself. We were not expecting to uncover any distinguishable features on a land mass as small as the Acropolis Hill. But there it was—in the location described in the *Critias*.

Not only is the formation a "low mountain" (300-500 feet)—just as Plato indicated—in the middle of the plain, but it is formed by two intersecting ridges that rise slowly and meet to form a cross-shaped hill. In other words, the centrally located hill divides the plain into four parts. This would have indeed served as a strategic spot to place the sacred temples since its summit is the highest point on the plain. If we encircle the two intersecting ridges, the area

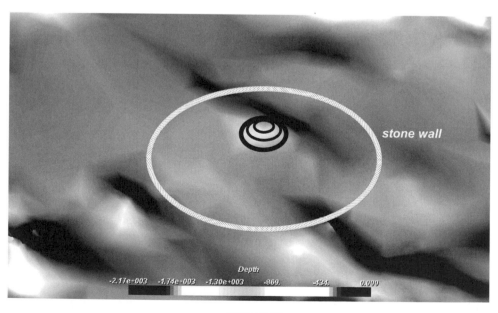

Figure 8:18
The Acropolis Hill as it would appear surrounded by a 14-mile-diameter wall.

becomes a cross within a circle, or a *pyramidal hill*—as if the valley is stamped with the very symbol of Atlantis!

In addition, other aspects of the physical dimensions of Atlantis City discussed in previous chapters can be correlated with what we believe to be the Acropolis Hill area on the seafloor.

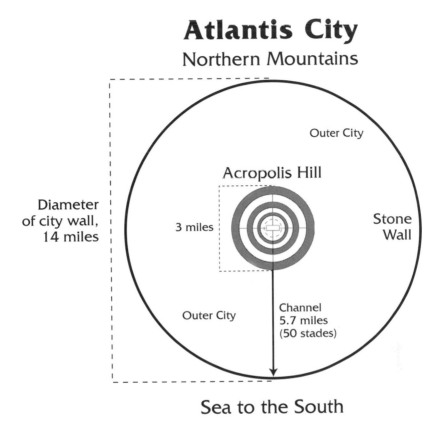

Figure 8:19
City plan of Atlantis.

As seen in Figure 8:19, the diameter of the stone wall that surrounded the circular city of Atlantis was about fourteen miles. The diameter of the Acropolis Hill itself was about three miles, and the length of the channel that was dug from the outermost ring to the southern sea was about fifty stades (almost six miles). Therefore, the temple area at the summit of the Acropolis Hill was about seven miles from the sea, which lay to the south.

The verification of these details was simple. Superimposing the plan of Atlantis City over bathymetric models of the submerged plain resulted in further support for our hypothesis. As seen in Figure 8:20, the fourteen-mile diameter of the stone wall that surrounded the city fits almost perfectly within the valley. The three concentric canals that surrounded the Acropolis Hill also fit around the central mound, which is just over seven miles from the southern sea. The match between details in the *Critias* concerning Atlantis City and our maps seemed to us just too close to be coincidental.

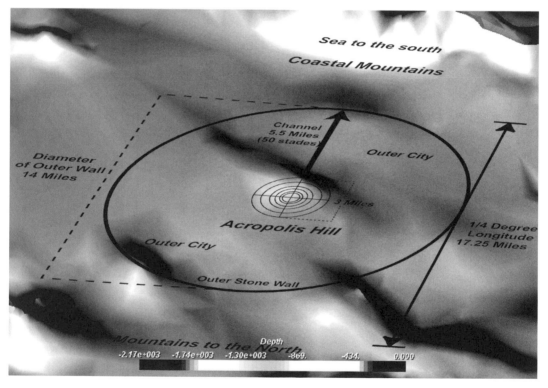

Figure 8:20
The city plan of Atlantis superimposed over the plain at the base of Cyprus, as seen looking south from the mountains to the north of the plain.

Tools and other artifacts excavated on Cyprus to date suggest that the earliest evidence of human habitation goes back at least 10,000 years.[11] But if we are right, there should be artifacts along this submerged portion of the Cyprus Arc that predate those on Cyprus's elevated surface. These questions will have to remain unanswered, however, until further explorations can, and likely will, be undertaken.

For the present, we are limited to the data at hand, but at least from this we can say that the bathymetric data fairly match Plato's account of Atlantis City and the Acropolis Hill.

Details of Atlantis City	Match with Cyprus
— Atlantis City was situated near the middle of the rectangular plain.	√
— The Acropolis Hill was a low mountain.	√
— The diameter of the circular outer stone wall that surrounded Atlantis City was 14 miles.	√
— The outer stone wall met the coastal hills of the southern sea and was about 7 miles from the Acropolis Hill.	√
— The diameter of the Acropolis Hill was 3 miles.	√

The Green Island of the Mediterranean Sea

Thus the whole day long till the setting of the sun the Olympians feasted, nor did their heart lack anything of the equal feast, nor of the beauteous lyre, that Apollo held, nor yet of the Muses, who sang, replying one to the other with sweet voices. But when the bright light of the sun was set, they went each to his own house to take their rest, where for each one a palace had been built....

— Homer
The Iliad (800 B.C.)

Our focus now shifts to the numerous clues Plato presented regarding the island's flora and fauna—its animal life, and the abundant natural resources for which Atlantis was famous.

Certainly, if we are hypothesizing that Atlantis was once contiguous with Cyprus, one would expect to find many of the natural features ascribed to Atlantis as belonging to Cyprus as well. Cyprus has always been very rich in timber and abundant natural resources, inspiring such references as "the Green Island of the Mediterranean Sea." Its vast and mountainous forests were plundered during the Bronze Age for construction but still remain rich in pine, cypress, and cedar trees. Home to an unusually large variety of plants and wild flowers, many of which cannot be found anywhere else in the world, the island has approximately 1,800 species and subspecies of flowering plants and is a major attraction for nature lovers, making it a botanist's paradise. The climate is mild and pleasant with over 300 sunny days a year.

As we know, Plato wrote of the rich botanical resources on Atlantis, with its roots, herbs, bushes, gums, cereals, pulse, oils, fruits and flowers.[12] Cyprus rests on a famous ophiolite complex with extremely rich soil. The foothills of the towering Troodos Massif have calcium-rich soils where carob and olive groves have flourished throughout the centuries. Indeed, Cyprus bears all the aromatic substances associated with Atlantis, as well an astonishing variety of products including resins, tannins, brushwood, charcoal, dyes, fibers, oaks, junipers, Judas Trees, Aleppo Pine, tree heather, fig trees, rosemary, sage, Spanish Broom, and erica species.

The nectars and ambrosia enjoyed by the citizens of Atlantis would have been found in abundance here. For a relatively small island, there are many varieties of vegetables as well as fruits such as lemons, oranges, grapefruits, tangerines, apples, peaches, pears, plums, cherries, melons, apricots, pomegranates, grapes, bananas, and dates. Pecans, hazelnuts, walnuts, almonds, and pine nuts are abundant. Cyprus also produces wheat and barley—grains which Isis and Osiris had supposedly found growing wild on their homeland and subsequently cultivated for the benefit of humanity.[13]

Cyprus's renewable forests could have produced the vast quantities of timber needed to build the Atlantean cities. Plato wrote that the Atlanteans used surrounding river systems to "float timber down from the mountains and transport seasonal produce by boat."[14]

As a rich and thriving economy bustling with the noise of merchants and manufacturers in its various cities and towns, the island of Atlantis also held abundant supplies of mineral resources, with extensive mining for both solid materials and precious metals. According to Plato, the huge circular walls that surrounded various sectors of Atlantis City were made of gold, silver, bronze, tin, and another metal unknown to us called "orichalc," which is often speculated to be golden-colored brass (copper and zinc). Atlantis has been especially linked with the mineral copper, however, because the island was said to be a vast storehouse of bronze, an alloy composed of ninety percent copper and ten percent tin. Many researchers also point to the fact that the name *Atlantis* seems to be related to South American names such as the Toltec *Atl,* meaning water, and the Peruvian *Anti,* meaning copper. Donnelly wrote: "…may it not be that the name of Atlantis is derived from these originals, and signified the copper island, or the copper mountains in the sea? And from these came the thousands of tons of copper and tin that must, during the Bronze Age, have been introduced into Europe?"[15]

In Hindu and Buddhist mythology we also find the legend of the earthly paradise associated with a copper mountain. The blue-colored figure of *Padmasambhava,* the "lotus born," is sometimes depicted on an island known as the "Glorious Copper Mountain Paradise" where he resides in the "Palace of Lotus Light." The three-storied palace/temple is encircled and protected by multiple walls and four gates where other deities stand guard for the "faraway pure land." He also holds a trident like Poseidon. This inner sanctum is identified with the summit of the famed Mt. Meru,[16] which has been, in turn, routinely associated with Atlantis. To this day many temples in that part of the world are adorned with copper roofs.

Among the many islands of the Mediterranean Sea, Cyprus is known to be one of the richest in metals.[17] The copper deposits on

Cyprus in particular were highly prized by the Egyptians, Phoenicians, Persians, Assyrians, Greeks, and Romans. In fact, the name Cyprus is synonymous with copper because "Cyprus was almost the sole source of copper to the Romans, who called it *aes cyprium* (ore of Cyprus), which was shortened to *cyprium* and later corrupted to *cuprum*. From this name comes the English name copper."[18] Consequently, the island of Cyprus in the eastern Mediterranean Sea certainly could be considered as the literal "copper mountain in the sea."

As we have seen, even Plato's reference to Atlantis's "numerous elephants," a topic that has perplexed Atlantis researchers worldwide, can be corroborated and matched with physical evidence found on Cyprus. Archeological excavations have uncovered fossil remains of dwarf elephants along with hippopotamuses that lived in the Kyrenia area some 11,000 years ago. There was also evidence that some of these bones exhibited cut marks associated with stone tools, indicating they were used as a human food resource. These discoveries on Cyprus support the notion that elephants were indeed present on the island, as Plato indicated.

We have now completed the list of identifying factors associated with Atlantis and matched them successfully with the island of Cyprus.

Details of Atlantis's Natural Resources	Match with Cyprus
— The island provided almost all the requirements for human life.	√
— The Atlanteans mined solid materials as well as various metals on the island.	√
— Atlantis had gold.	√
— Atlantis had silver.	√
— Atlantis had copper.	√
— Atlantis had tin.	√
— Atlantis had precious stones.	√
— Timber was plentiful.	√
— Atlantis had black, yellow, and white rocks (marble) that were used for construction.	√

- Atlantis abounded with roots, herbs, bushes, gums, fruits, and flowers. √
- There were crops, cereals, pulse, and oils in "wonderful quality and profusion." √
- There were elephants on the island. √

Garden of Eden?

The Lord God planted a garden eastward in Eden, and there
He put the man whom He had formed. And out of the ground the
Lord God made every tree grow that is pleasant to the sight and
good for food. The tree of life was also in the midst of the garden, and
the tree of the knowledge of good and evil. Now a river went out of Eden
to water the garden, and from there it parted and became four riverheads.

— Genesis 2: 8-10

A variety of researchers, including Ignatius Donnelly, have endeavored to link the legend of Atlantis with the biblical account of the Garden of Eden. For those who have thoroughly studied the subject, there is a clear suspicion that the biblical Eden and Atlantis are different stories describing the same prehistoric set of events. For example, a study of Sumerian texts, written thousands of years before the compilation of the Old Testament, reveals that the name Eden itself comes from the Sumerian *E.din,* which simply means "fertile plain."

Connections between Eden and Atlantis have even been suggested for New World Mesoamerican cultures. According to Donnelly, "not only do we find this tradition of the Garden of Eden in the Old World, but it meets us also among the civilized races of America. The elder Montezuma said to Cortez, 'Our fathers dwelt in that happy and prosperous place which they called Aztlan, which means whiteness. . . . In this place there is a great mountain in the middle of the water which is called Culhuacan, because it has the point somewhat turned over toward the bottom; and for this cause it is called Culhuacan, which means 'crooked mountain.' "[19] Our models show the Troodos Massif and its towering Mt. Olympus, Cyprus's highest peak, as indeed "somewhat turned over toward the bottom." Looking back at the images, it is at least possible that in its antediluvian form Cyprus could have been viewed as a "crooked mountain."

Central to our case, however, are the more directly concrete, empirical indicators of an Atlantis/Eden connection. In Genesis, Eden is reported to have had a "river that went out of it." This seems to suggest a continuity of land between Eden and other places, and not merely a river terminating at a discharge point into the sea. If Atlantis referred to the same place as Eden, then Atlantis must also have had a river running out of it, and, if so, it must have been joined to a continental landmass. This inference is quite convenient for us to check out, because, for our Atlantis, there was only one small land exit—over the isthmus at the Syrian coastline.

As described earlier, the 3D models do indeed indicate the presence of a land bridge (the Tartus Ridge) that connects the submarine valley with the coast of northern Syria. In its state prior to the great flood, the isthmus is shown to be rather concave and narrow; if in fact Atlantis discharged a river to the continent, it would have to have flowed through this narrow bridge to present-day Syria. Thus, adding this important component to our list of corroborating facts should be relatively straightforward.

Required, of course, was evidence of a possible river connection from the Syrian coastline to the West Tartus Ridge. As it turns out, there is indeed a rather nice alignment of the Kabir River with the Tartus Ridge. The Kabir runs through the highlands of northern Syria, just south of the city of Latakia. While our models do not reveal the kind of detail required to locate ancient river channels, it is reasonable to postulate a Kabir River–Tartus Ridge continuity. The river presently forms part of the border between

Syria and Lebanon as it cuts through the massive mountain range. The Arabic name for Kabir River, *Nahr al Kabir,* actually translates to "the Great River," the same name it may have carried since the days of Eden.

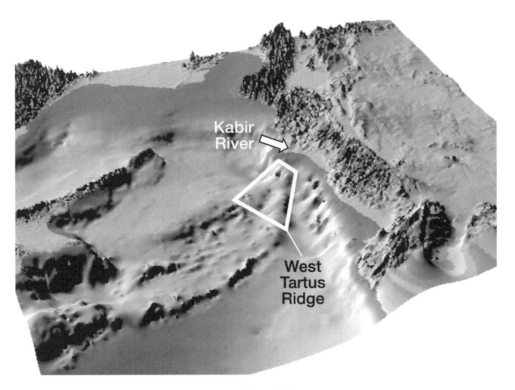

Figure 8:21
The Kabir River on Syria's mainland is aligned
with the submerged West Tartus Ridge.

Figure 8:21 illustrates the location of the riverbed on the Syrian mainland which meets the Tartus Ridge at the coastline. In this view, the arrow points to the river path as it extends eastward from the Syrian coastline and cuts through the mountain range where it meets the Ghab Depression, a forty-mile longitudinal trench that contains the valley of the Orontes River. Today this ancient river runs westward and empties into the Mediterranean, but prior to the sinking of the Mediterranean Basin it would have flowed out of Atlantis/Eden through the peninsular neck. From here it would have entered the eastern mainland where it coursed through the coastal mountains of Syria before turning south. From there, as it says in Genesis, "it parted and became four riverheads," one of which was probably the Euphrates River.

This area is the source of a number of very ancient artifacts and beliefs. Just a short distance from the city of Latakia lie the ancient ruins of Ugarit, recognized as one of the world's oldest settlements. The Ras Shamra texts relating to the infamous god Baal, or "He Who Rides on Clouds," were found here. It is also the site where archeologists uncovered evidence of the oldest alphabet ever found on earth, made of molded clay and engraved with cuneiform signs on a finger-sized rod. It is currently exhibited at the Damascus Museum.

Carried by the Phoenicians, this alphabet contained thirty cuneiform letters and was adopted by the Greeks, the Etruscans, and the Romans—the same alphabet that is used today by a large number of the peoples of the world. The letters are A, B, C, D, E, H, I, K, L, M, N, O, P, Q, R, S, T and Z.[20] It could be said that we are indebted to the Phoenicians, and perhaps further, to the Atlanteans, for the majority of our alphabet. Donnelly wrote: "We shall find, as we proceed, that the Phoenicians were unquestionably identified with Atlantis, and that it was probably from Atlantis they derived their god Baal. . . ."[21]

The legend of Atlantis comes to us through the filter of Plato's writing, and perhaps this makes the Atlanteans seem rather "Greek-like." To the Egyptians they may have appeared more Egyptian, and to the Hebrews, the "mighty men of old" may have seemed more religious and patriarchal. When we strip away all the cultural nuances however, we are left with a legend of a highly advanced civilization existing in the eastern Mediterranean region—a civilization that long predates even ancient societies, and one supposedly organized at higher levels of development, especially in regard to knowledge, spirituality, and technology.

Has Atlantis been here all along, deep in the heart of the ancient world and just a few miles from Egypt and Greece? How much more evidence do we need before we consider this discovery as a very real possibility?

It would indeed be ironic if perhaps the greatest mystery of all time were solved by taking *literally* the words of the man who was perhaps the greatest philosopher of all time.

Epilogue

We are on the threshold. Scientific investigation is advancing with great strides. Who shall say that one hundred years from now the great museums of the world may not be adorned with gems, statues, arms, and implements from Atlantis, while the libraries of the world shall contain translations of its inscriptions, throwing new light upon all the past history of the human race, and all the great problems which now perplex the thinkers of the day?

— Ignatius Donnelly
Atlantis: The Antediluvian World (1882)

Three long years have passed since I first laid eyes on what I believe to be the Plain of Atlantis, and all the research and painstaking analyses since that memorable day have only served to further substantiate the possibility of that discovery. It has truly been an astonishing experience throughout.

This work has utilized new sonar data to depict the actual topographic conditions of the eastern Mediterranean seafloor, which were discussed within the context of a general search for Atlantis. The bathymetric maps, according to our interpretations, support the hypothesis that Atlantis actually existed and was located in the proximity of Cyprus. The matches with Plato's account are simply too numerous to be coincidental.

This study stands apart from other Atlantis theories mainly because our apparent discovery is supported by hard data. The configuration located at 34.8° N, 35° E, and highlighted in our images of the seafloor (the pyramidal elevation and its nearby formations), is suggested as belonging to the Acropolis Hill of Atlantis. To my knowledge, no other competing theories have been able to make such a claim.

I believe that the hypothesis offered here is valid according to scientific standards, but only further investigations under the sediment cover will verify or invalidate the claim. My own feelings leave little room for doubt, but I have endeavored to remain critical; nevertheless, I feel compelled to express my belief that below the blue waters of the eastern Mediterranean Sea, just a few thousand feet below the surface, the treasure of the ages awaits discovery.

The discovery of Atlantis/Eden is one of those events that may well change history as we presently understand it. Of course, it is a given that new discoveries that have the potential to change humanity's conception of reality routinely confront obstacles such as hardened skeptics and dogmatic incredulity. I would argue that not only is the hypothesis valid enough to warrant an investigation, its implications are too important to be ignored. Given its potential to restructure existing models of history, cultural evolution, and perhaps even the foundation of the world's leading religions, this area of the world—never before seen by human eyes—should be promptly examined. After all, space may be the final frontier, but there are many uncharted frontiers remaining right here on earth, some of which may be far more worthy of examination, given their potential impact on human knowledge.

The ancients believed that the demise of Atlantis marked the end of an era on earth—the Golden Age, when gods dwelled among humanity and ruled according to the wisdom of heaven. The destruction of the Garden also marked the beginning of what was considered to be the great dark ages for the human race, which continues to flounder amidst warring religious, political, and economic factions. Discovering the remains of Atlantis will be analogous to recovering a repressed memory from the depths of humanity's unconscious mind. In our present state, we collectively suffer the fate of an unfortunate soul with amnesia, utterly unaware of our past. Finding the long-lost civilization of

Atlantis will undoubtedly be as shocking, and healing, as the dawning of memory would be for our amnesiac patient.

When the real, practical problems of continuing this investigation are considered, we seem to be facing quite favorable conditions. With no sunlight, heat, oxygen, or wind to degrade its remains, Atlantis would be mummified in the cold waters of the deep sea, frozen in time. The stone walls of Atlantis as well as the gigantic structures on the summit of the Acropolis Hill would be preserved and should be easily accessible. Very little sedimentation occurs in the deep-sea areas of the Mediterranean, and with the target area resting far from shore in international waters, a few inches of accumulated sediment would fail to hide the remains of an entire city. There are colossal buildings, bridges, roads, canals, stone temples, and ancient artifacts to be found.

So, here we are at a critical juncture. We have presented a case for the location of Atlantis using historical sources such as the writing of Plato, and we have supported the case with concrete, corroborating evidence. Determining the final truth or falsity of our claims now rests with the acquisition of more detailed maps and the application of deep-sea technologies. While certainly challenging, the task of conducting seafloor exploration is relatively uncomplicated. If the Titanic, a comparatively small target, could be found and explored two miles below the icy Atlantic waters, then locating the remains of a whole city at depths of less than one mile should be far less problematic.

In the last few decades, deep-sea research has become far more sophisticated and affordable. High-resolution maps and even picture-like images of the possible targets can be accomplished with sonar. Targets of opportunity could then be further explored with a modern Remote Operated Vehicle (ROV), which could be employed to remove sediment, to videotape, and to possibly salvage artifacts. All that would be needed is simple videotape footage showing megalithic stone structures on the seafloor, dozens of miles from shore. Certainly, the possibility of such

Figure E:1
An example of what waits to be found on the seafloor today.

a tantalizing discovery is too great to resist given the relative simplicity of the effort.

It has been almost 2,400 years since Plato wrote about a lost civilization he referred to as Atlantis. We may soon be able to write about real artifacts from the prehistoric Atlantean culture and at long last solve the greatest mystery on earth. I truly believe that the dawn of a new era is at hand.

Robert Sarmast
July 6, 2003

DiscoveryofAtlantis.com

Expedition Report

By Commodore Robert S. Bates

April 2006

In July of 2002, Robert Sarmast assembled a team of profession-als from various disciplines to pursue his vision of verifying the location of Atlantis, which he had evolved through extensive academic research. Some professionals were already on board when, as an independent maritime consultant, I was contacted and asked to provide the quality assurance and navigational accuracy of the planned activities in connection with the first expedition to the designated site. With a maritime background that spans a half century and experience on survey and research vessels, it was a good fit, particularly due to my insistence on the protection of intellectual property and the precision with which the naviga-tional and scientific data needed to be documented. It was also my track record in academia, spanning thirty-five years, which insured an objective report at the end of the voyage.

Like any scientific experiment, the exact methods used, the equipment employed and integrity of the data must be docu-mented to be considered valid. With the methodology and data completely disclosed, any other researcher is at liberty to conduct the same procedure. If it results in the same conclusions, there is good reason to believe that the findings have been verified.

Robert Sarmast strictly adhered to the maritime protocol associated with this kind of research. The independent company contracted to provide the sonar technicians and the associated equipment was Phoenix International of Landover, MD. The ship used, the FLYING ENTERPRISE, Official IMO Number 7212482, is owned and operated by EDT Towage and Salvage Company, Ltd. of Limassol, Cyprus. It is essentially a medium size research vessel, although it could also be used for commercial towing and salvage work.

It was in excellent condition for the voyage and had all the modern navigational equipment necessary to provide precise and reliable expedition data. Ship's positions and tracklines were determined by differential GPS providing utmost accuracy. The ship's master was Captain Duncan MacKenzie.

The initial survey plan was based on the bathymetric multi-beam scans conducted by the Russian academician Andrei L. Knipper from the Russian survey vessel AKADEMIK NIKOLAJ STRAKHOV in 1987 and 1990. In 1994, the data were made available to the international community in a research paper by Dr. John K. Hall addressing the bottom relief of the Levantine Sea. The topography was indistinct at best, and the navigation associated with the data was somewhat suspect. Nevertheless, based on that preliminary data, a position of the central area of exploration was estimated by Robert Sarmast to be in the vicinity of 34.8° N, 35.0° E. From the Russian survey, the general topography of the survey area was determined to a centrally located oblong mound or hill, approximately 100 meters high, approximately 2.8 kilometers long by approximately 600 meters wide. The hill is bordered by a relatively flat plain with low hills to the north and south.

In July 2004, nautical charts from both the British Admiralty (UK) and the National Oceanographic and Atmospheric Administration (US) were consulted in an effort to verify the central position. The chart analysis, with only relatively few soundings, still indicated that the central elevated target area appeared to be located at 34.8°N, 35.0°E. The position was predicated on what appeared to be the presence of an elevated ridge that ran through the central sector from Syria toward a point south of Cyprus. The contour lines also followed a general NE-SW pattern. Later in July of 2004, through a contact that Robert Sarmast made with a principal investigator from the Institut Français de Recherche pour l'Exploitation de la Mer (IFRE-MER), more definitive data, with better navigational information, was requested for an area fifteen nautical miles square around the central hill. The request for bathymetric data covered an area in the form of a square with coordinates (34°58.5'N, 34°51.9'E), (34°58.5'N, 35°10.2'E), (34°43.5'N, 35°10.2'E), (34°43.5'N, 34°51.9'E). The area needed only a portion of the data taken from the bathymetric multibeam sonar survey by the French Research Vessel (R/V) LE SUROîT during a voyage from October 29 to November 15, 2003. During that expedition, two scientific subjects were under study for IFREMER. The first topic was the geodynamics of a convergent/transcurrent system in the zone-relay between the Arc of Cyprus and the Is–Anatolian fault. The structure of this zone and its geodynamic evolution, under the influence of the movements of three plates, were under consideration. The second topic related to sedimentary dynamics, in those two areas of seabed, generated by the activity of the arc of Cyprus and the activity along the Levantine continental terrace. The acquisition of bathymetry and the acoustic reflectivity data were an integral part of their research. Since the request from Robert Sarmast was specifically for marine archeological research, and was not related to either of the IFREMER studies, the request was granted.

On September 1, 2004, Robert Sarmast received the request-ed data from IFREMER and he forwarded it to the Scotia Group in Dallas, Texas who returned three dimensional (3-D) proprietary graphic modeling software supporting Robert Sarmast's claim of the existence of structures in that area. The 3-D graphic display model of the data provided imagery appearing to be a 3700 meters long, nine meters tall, straight wall structure to the north and a 2800 meters long, by 500-800 meters wide, irregular tabu-lar structure on a low, 110 meters high hill, to the south. Also in evidence were canal-like ducts near the top of the low hill that led off the hill on the north side. It also appeared that an ancient river bed may have meandered along the south side of the hill. The remains of a ridge, on either side of, and adjoining the central hill, about a mile wide at the widest point, divides the survey area into two parts; a northwestern section and a southeastern section. The ridge is in line with, and connects to, the central hill and is formed in a direction that roughly follows a NE-SW axis through the central hill. It was this pattern that dictated the deployment and operation of side scan sonar along course lines over the site. The portion of the ridge to the northeast of the central mound is the most pronounced. The ridge to the southwest of the central mound terminates in a mud volcano a little more than six miles from the central hill. Other reports indicate that the area is prone to the formation of mud volcanoes; however, the central oblong hill did not resemble the volcanoes in this, or any other, area. The nature of the bottom is unknown, but a survey in adjacent areas indicates the possibility of a silted clay bottom. From the new bathymetric maps, it was reasonable to assume that megalithic stones or megalithic stone structures could be present in the survey area especially on and around the central sector. None of these features were evident in the earlier multibeam scans from the Russian vessel AKADEMIK NIKOLAJ STRAKHOV.

With the position, topography and orientation of the site well defined by the IFREMER data, the basis for the expedition and the plan for a detailed examination with side scan sonar emerged. Where multibeam sonar presents images from the bottom of the survey vessel, in this case, a mile above the target, side scan sonar can be used at great depths in close proximity to the survey area and it is one of the best systems for imaging large areas of the ocean floor. The basic concept is much the same as the basic echo sounder; however, the side scan sonar instrument is towed behind a ship and is often called a towfish or a tow vehicle. This technology uses a specially shaped acoustic beam, which pulses out 90 degrees from the path on which it is towed, and out to each side. Each pulse contributes to a detailed image of a narrow strip directly to either side of the instrument. The topography of the ocean floor and underwater objects reflect the sound energy to hydrophones on the tow vehicle. These reflections are amplified, processed and displayed as images. The instrument by which this mission area was surveyed was a modified GeoAcoustics 941 Transceiver and 942 Subsea multiplexor mounted on a Geo-Acoustics 136 Towfish. The tow cable was 5500m of Rochester A302799 11.3mm double armored coax. Each track of side scan sonar was recorded by the CODA sys dualSense processor from Coda Technologies. All equipment was calibrated and performed reliably throughout the exploration. Project manager Tim Weller led the Phoenix International sonar team. Under the voyage plan, initially two side scan swaths were conducted along the northern wall, historically, the first side scan swaths to record the nature of the stone structure. With a fairly regular bottom, the initial swaths went smoothly, with the towfish maneuvering approximately 20 meters above the targeted wall.

At the conclusion of the two side scan passes over the mega-lithic wall, the towfish cable was shortened to 2,400 meters. During a torrential downpour from a passing rain cell, an accidental flooding and shorting of the deck generator associated with the sonar winch assembly rendered the winch inoperable by any means, and the towfish was perilously deployed with no mechanical means to shorten the tow cable or bring the towfish aboard. Maneuvering the towfish toward a rendezvous point near Cyprus enabled a correction of the problem when the M/V EDT ARES, also operated by EDT Towage and Salvage Company, Ltd. delivered a replacement generator. The evolution took 21 hours and 24 minutes from the time the first generator quit, to the running of the replacement generator.

Returning to the area of investigation, redeployment of the towfish enabled scans over the low hill. Seven scans were conducted over the hill and a third line was conducted over the wall to gain greater coverage of the megalithic wall structure. When the data was returned in the form of visual strips showing the survey progress with the on-screen monitor in real-time, it became evident that the position which Robert Sarmast had predicted was accurate. Subsequently, mosaics of multiple passes by the side scan sonar were produced by combining adjacent strips to give the final pictures of his discovery.

If the side scan sonar mosaics were combined with the IFREMER multibeam picture of the hill, the IFREMER profiles and elevations match nicely with the side scan data to present a partial picture of the upper portion of the hill. What appear to be the features of two semi-circular canals in the side scan images are located where canal-like ducts appeared in the less detailed IFREMER multibeam scans. There is also an indication that, what appears to be a section of a third circular canal segment, also exists. Other smaller details in the side scan images give rise to the conjecture that other structures have also been detected, which need to be examined more closely for identification and classification. Although the site was certainly deteriorated by the ravages of time, the Sarmast Expedition in 2004 captured enough of the detail near the top if the hill and the wall at the base to finally give a much better sense of its layout for reconciliation and comparison with the various verbal accounts of this lost civilization.

The first voyage to this site, specifically for the archeological study, was made possible by the hard work and sacrifice of a large number of outstanding individuals. Thanks to their efforts, the release of the first side scan images of this historic site present the most credible evidence of man-quarried and man-built mega-lithic structures, the remains of which are consistent with measurements and descriptions of various documented sources. From a scientific and archeological prospective, the first voyage was an unprecedented success of enormous historical value. With over a decade of research and publishing by Robert Sarmast, coupled with over two years of planning by him and his team, the first expedition has indeed brought the debate over its existence closer to a conclusion than ever before and has established the foundation for further monumental discoveries.

Robert Sarmast, the Principle Investigator and Expedition Director, requested that I take on the duties of expedition leader to insure the success and validity of the maritime aspects of his project. Assuming the role of Commodore, I prepared a lengthy post-expedition report, the highlights of which are incorporated here. Among other considerations, the report certifies the accuracy of his discovery and provides a paper trail for historical documentation and subsequent endeavors to explore the site. With the documentation of this voyage, the world can not only trust his claim, but it can also verify it at will.

Commodore Robert Stanley Bates, USMM
Expedition Leader

Acknowledgments

This work would have been impossible to produce were it not for the generous support of dozens of individuals who came forward to help in the last few years. It is hardly possible to name them all and give proper thanks for everything they have contributed. Looking back, there is no doubt in my mind that each of these individuals played a vital role in bringing about the production of this book.

In particular, I would like to thank Marielle and my family, for putting up with the enormous pressure that was created in our lives by undertaking this colossal challenge, and for giving me the strength and resolve to bring things to fruition. I thank Michael Wisenbaker for his generosity in funding the mapping of the eastern Mediterranean Basin and giving me all the expertise, knowledge, and tools necessary to get the job done. I am also eternally indebted to my original publisher, editor, agent, and friend, Byron ("the Steadfast") Belitsos, who stood by me from the very beginning and gave me unlimited access to his remarkable talents in producing a fine literary work. Many thanks to Fred Harris, Harry McMullan, and Capt. Robert Bates for providing technical support and financial help.

I was fortunate to get help from a wonderful team of editors and proofers who gave so much of their time and energy to get this book finished: George Marsh, Brian Sikorski, Marty Eigenberger, Victoria Louise Clark, and Mary Elaine Ware. Many thanks also to Bill Dixon, Nena Norwood, Saskia Raevouri, and Matthew Block. It was an honor to have several artists contributing to the project: Phillip Dizick designed and produced the interior and the book cover I always dreamed of; Bo Atkinson recreated the Acropolis Hill and brought Atlantis back to life through his images; Freydoon Rassouli gave us his beautiful painting of the birth of Aphrodite.

On the technical side of things, I would like to thank Patrick Lowry at the Scotia Group for providing his nearly magical talents in producing the maps, 3D models, and special software programs that allowed us to get the world's first detailed peek at the Cyprus Arc, and to accurately depict the eastern Mediterranean Sea at different sea levels. I will also always treasure my contacts with Dr. John K. Hall of the Geological Survey of Israel, whose research alongside the Geological Institute of the Russian Academy of Sciences served as the foundation for our mapmaking process. And I would have never found this research had it not been for a fortunate meeting with the caring team of David Cole and John Campagnoli at the National Geophysical Data Center (NOAA) in Boulder, Colorado, who gave me access to the precious raw data necessary to create our maps.

Finally, I would like to express my thanks for the gracious help of many people who came forward to lend a hand when I needed it most: Janelle Balnicke, Jerry Dalton, Brian Smith, Neda Sarmast, Rob Davis, Dennis de Jong, Paul Anderson, Larry and Joan Mullins, Don Green, Paula Thompson, Yves Vincent, Brigitte Mars and Tom Pfeiffer, Paul Buttitta, Les Rogers, Alex Brosgart, Dick and Peggy Johnson, Rosey Lieske, Robert and Linda Buselli, Carol Kline, Eve McMahon, Lee and Millie Maxton, Gerry Johnson, and Ingrid Alonso.

Post-expedition Salute

It is literally true that it took dozens of people to launch this project and organize the expedition, and each of them played an indispensable role. A few incredible souls, however, seem to have been sent straight from heaven to keep me on track. Words cannot express my appreciation for the tireless efforts of Fred Harris Jr. (company attorney), Gerald Dalton (company treasurer), Byron Belitsos (company secretary), Commodore Robert S. Bates (expedition leader), Dennis de Jong (webmaster), Saskia Raevouri (fundraiser), Janelle Balnicke (film producer), Angela Henderson (publicist), and Axel Schoeller (diver).

I express my sincere gratitude to the government of Cyprus for supporting this project and welcoming me with true Cypriot hospitality. Special thanks go to Mr. Andreas Kyprianides, Mr. Yiorgos Lillikas, Mr. Photis Photiou, Mr. Michalis Metaxas, Mr. Krinos Hadjigeorgiou, Mr. Neophytos Christodou, Mr. Christos Moustras, and everyone at the Cyprus Tourism Organization.

Many thanks to Colin Wilson for having the courage to be an outsider; Darios Melas and the EDT team; Captain Duncan MacKenzie; Captain Dionisios Tritsapolis; Steve Saint-Amour and Tim Weller and the Phoenix team; Russell Dodd and Stan Moroney of GSE; Jean-Raphael Dedieu and the Redwood Studio team; Mark Greer; Angelo Ioannou; Panikos Christophorou; Group Captain Nick C. Randle (RAF); Chrissie Flint; Justin E. Manley; Vassos Pantelas; Philippos Droushiotis; Antonis Kyriakides; Kyriakos Kyriakou; Chris Kowal; Bart Noonan; Tracy Pattin and the Video Box team; Tim Beacham and Natalie Morales of NBC; Pedram and Pejman and Sally Moosavizadeh; Otis and Hugo; Christina Sekeris; Drew Levin and the TMC team; Dr. Yu Pashkov; Nicos Nicolau; Vladimir Dyokin; and the Psichogios family. Most of all I am deeply indebted to Ambassador Andros Nicolaides and his wife Ero, and especially Melina, for doing so much to help me and to see this project succeed.

Of course, none of this could have happened without the monetary support of those who invested in First Source Enterprises, LLC, and made the expedition possible: Jean Ascher, Paul Anderson, Nicholas Avalos, Janelle Balnicke, Byron Belitsos, George Benavides, Michael Bertola, Paul Buttitta, Phil Calabrese, Tom Choquette, Victoria Clark, Ron Cyr, Gerald Dalton, Dennis de Jong, Mary Jo Garascia, Larry Geis, Ron & Cathy Harrell, Fred Harris Jr., Normalinda Hays, Barbara Hester, Gard Jameson, Nancy Johnson, Dick & Peggy Johnson, Halbert Katzen, Lucille Kettell, Robert & Beverly Lawson, Lyn & Norman Lear, Steve & Diane Lewis, Marcia Lynch, Martin Turner & Paula Maas, Eric Maichak, Chick Montgomery, Robert O'Guin, Joseph Pattin, Richard Poitevin, Valerie Potter, Saskia Raevouri, John & Jane Roper, Brian Sikorski, Gordon Snell, Mark & Charrie Stump, Waldine Stump, George Thornbury, Grant & Liz Walmouth, Bruce & Beth Wenger, Larry & Donna Whelan, Jo Ann Wiedman, and Hollis Williams. Last but not least, I wish to thank the scores of individuals whose heartfelt supplementary contributions gave the expedition a wide support base that goes beyond money.

Thank you all!

Appendix

Note: The short excerpts from Plato's Timaeus and Critias provided below are to familiarize the reader with the original description of the lost island of Atlantis. Although it is mentioned only briefly in the Timaeus, Atlantis takes center stage in the Critias. The public-domain translation by Benjamin Jowett in this Appendix is slightly different from the Desmond Lee translation quoted in the chapters of this book.

Timaeus

Egyptian priest, speaking to Solon (Timaeus 24e-25d):

"Many great and wonderful deeds are recorded of your state in our histories. But one of them exceeds all the rest in greatness and valour. For these histories tell of a mighty power which unprovoked made an expedition against the whole of Europe and Asia, and to which your city put an end. This power came forth out of the Atlantic Ocean, for in those days the Atlantic was navigable; and there was an island situated in front of the straits which are by you called the Pillars of Heracles; the island was larger than Libya and Asia put together, and was the way to other islands, and from these you might pass to the whole of the opposite continent which surrounded the true ocean; for this sea which is within the Straits of Heracles is only a harbour, having a narrow entrance, but that other is a real sea, and the surrounding land may be most truly called a boundless continent.

Now in this island of Atlantis there was a great and wonderful empire which had rule over the whole island and several others, and over parts of the continent, and, furthermore, the men of Atlantis had subjected the parts of Libya within the columns of Heracles as far as Egypt, and of Europe as far as Tyrrhenia. This vast power, gathered into one, endeavoured to subdue at a blow our country and yours and the whole of the region within the straits; and then, Solon, your country shone forth, in the excellence of her virtue and strength, among all mankind. She was pre-eminent in courage and military skill, and was the leader of the Hellenes. And when the rest fell off from her, being compelled to stand alone, after having undergone the very extremity of danger, she defeated and triumphed over the invaders, and preserved from slavery those who were not yet subjugated, and generously liberated all the rest of us who dwell within the pillars.

But afterwards there occurred violent earthquakes and floods; and in a single day and night of misfortune all your warlike men in a body sank into the earth, and the island of Atlantis in like manner disappeared in the depths of the sea. For which reason the sea in those parts is impassable and impenetrable, because there is a shoal of mud in the way; and this was caused by the subsidence of the island."

Critias

Critias speaking to Socrates, Hermocrates, and Timaeus (Critias 113-121):

". . . Before proceeding further in the narrative, I ought to warn you, that you must not be surprised if you should perhaps hear Hellenic names given to foreigners. I will tell you the reason of this: Solon, who was intending to use the tale for his poem, enquired into the meaning of the names, and found that the early Egyptians in writing them down had translated them into their own language, and he recovered the meaning of the several names and when copying them out again translated them into our language. My great-grandfather, Dropides, had the original writing, which is still in my possession, and was carefully studied by me when I was a child. Therefore if you hear names such as are used in this country, you must not be surprised, for I have told how they came to be introduced. The tale, which was of great length, began as follows:

I have before remarked in speaking of the allotments of the gods, that they distributed the whole earth into portions differing in extent, and made for themselves temples and instituted sacrifices. And Poseidon, receiving for his lot the island of Atlantis, begat children by a mortal woman, and settled them in a part of the island, which I will describe. Looking towards the sea, but in the centre of the whole island, there was a plain which is said to have been the fairest of all plains and very fertile. Near the plain again, and also in the centre of the island at a distance of about fifty stadia, there was a mountain not very high on any side.

In this mountain there dwelt one of the earth born primeval men of that country, whose name was Evenor, and he had a wife named Leucippe, and they had an only daughter who was called Cleito. The maiden had already reached womanhood, when her father and mother died; Poseidon fell in love with her and had intercourse with her, and breaking the ground, inclosed the hill in which she dwelt all round, making alternate zones of sea and land larger and smaller, encircling one another; there were two of land and three of water, which he turned as with a lathe, each having its circumference equidistant every way from the centre, so that no man could get to the island, for ships and voyages were not as yet. He himself, being a god, found no difficulty in making special arrangements for the centre island, bringing up two springs of water from beneath the earth, one of warm water and the other of cold, and making every variety of food to spring up abundantly from the soil. He also begat and brought up five pairs of twin male children; and dividing the island of Atlantis into ten portions, he gave to the first-born of the eldest pair his mother's dwelling and the surrounding allotment, which was the largest and best, and made him king over the rest; the others he made princes, and gave them rule over many men, and a large territory. And he named them all; the eldest, who was the first king, he named Atlas, and after him the whole island and the ocean were called Atlantic. To his twin brother, who was born after him, and obtained as his lot the extremity of the island towards the Pillars of Heracles, facing the country which is now called the region of Gades in that part of the world, he gave the name which in the Hellenic language is Eumelus, in the language of the country which is named after him, Gadeirus. Of the second pair of twins he called one Ampheres, and the other Evaemon. To the elder of the third pair of twins he gave the name Mneseus, and Autochthon to the one who followed him. Of the fourth pair of twins he called the elder Elasippus, and the younger Mestor. And of the fifth pair he gave to the elder the name of Azaes, and to the younger that of Diaprepes. All these and their descendants for many generations were the inhabitants and rulers of divers islands in the open sea; and also, as has been already said, they held sway in our direction over the country within the Pillars as far as Egypt and Tyrrhenia.

Now Atlas had a numerous and honourable family, and they retained the kingdom, the eldest son handing it on to his eldest for many generations; and they had such an amount of wealth as was never before possessed by kings and potentates, and is not likely ever to be again, and they were furnished with everything which they needed, both in the city and country. For because of the greatness of their empire many things were brought to them from foreign countries, and the island itself provided most of what was required by them for the uses of life. In the first place, they dug out of the earth whatever was to be found there, solid as well as fusile, and that which is now only a name and was then something more than a name, orichalcum, was dug out of the earth in many parts of the island, being more precious in those days than anything except gold. There was an abundance of wood for carpenter's work, and sufficient maintenance for tame and wild animals. Moreover, there were a great number of elephants in the island; for as there was provision for all other sorts of animals, both for those which live in lakes and marshes and rivers, and also for those which live in mountains and on plains, so there was for the animal which is the largest and most voracious of all. Also whatever fragrant things there now are in the earth, whether roots, or herbage, or woods, or essences which distil from fruit and flower, grew and thrived in that land; also the fruit which admits of cultivation, both the dry sort, which is given us for nourishment and any other which we use for food-we call them all by the common name pulse, and the fruits having a hard rind, affording drinks and meats and ointments, and good store of chestnuts and the like, which furnish pleasure and amusement, and are fruits which spoil with keeping, and the pleasant kinds of dessert, with which we console ourselves after dinner, when we are tired of eating-all these that sacred island which then beheld the light of the sun, brought forth fair and wondrous and in infinite abundance. With such blessings the earth freely furnished them; meanwhile they went on constructing their temples and palaces and harbours and docks. And they arranged the whole country in the following manner:

First of all they bridged over the zones of sea which surrounded the ancient metropolis, making a road to and from the royal palace. And at the very beginning they built the palace in the habitation of the god and of their ancestors, which they continued to ornament in successive generations, every king surpassing the one who went before him to the utmost of his power, until they made the building a marvel to behold for size and for beauty. And beginning from the sea they bored a canal of three hundred feet in width and one hundred feet in depth and fifty stadia in length, which they carried through to the outermost zone, making a passage from the sea up to this, which became a harbour, and leaving an opening sufficient to enable the largest vessels to find ingress. Moreover, they divided at the bridges the zones of land which parted the zones of sea, leaving room for a single trireme to pass out of one zone into another, and they covered over the channels so as to leave a way underneath for the ships; for the banks were raised considerably above the water. Now the largest of the zones into which a passage was cut from the sea was three stadia in breadth, and the zone of land which came next of equal breadth; but the next two zones, the one of water, the other of land, were two stadia, and the one which surrounded the central island was a stadium only in width. The island in which the palace was situated had a diameter of five stadia. All this including the zones and the bridge, which was the sixth part of a stadium in width, they surrounded by a stone wall on every side, placing towers and gates on the bridges where the sea passed in. The stone which was used in the work they quarried from underneath the centre island, and from underneath the zones, on the outer as well as the inner side. One kind was white, another black, and a third red, and as they quarried, they at the same time hollowed out double docks, having roofs formed out of the native rock. Some of their buildings were simple, but in others they put together different stones, varying the colour to please the eye, and to be a natural source of delight. The entire circuit of the wall, which went round the outermost zone, they covered with a coating of brass, and the circuit of the next wall they coated with tin, and the third, which encompassed the citadel, flashed with the red light of orichalcum.

The palaces in the interior of the citadel were constructed on this wise: in the centre was a holy temple dedicated to Cleito and Poseidon, which remained inaccessible, and was surrounded by an enclosure of gold; this was the spot where the family of the ten princes first saw the light, and thither the people annually brought the fruits of the earth in their season from all the ten portions, to be an offering to each of the ten. Here was Poseidon's own temple which was a stadium in length, and half a stadium in width, and of a proportionate height, having a strange barbaric appearance. All the outside of the temple, with the exception of the pinnacles, they covered with silver, and the pinnacles with gold. In the interior of the temple the roof was of ivory, curiously wrought everywhere with gold and silver and orichalcum; and all the other parts, the walls and pillars and floor, they coated with orichalcum. In the temple they placed statues of gold: there was the god himself standing in a chariot-the charioteer of six winged horses-and of such a size that he touched the roof of the building with his head; around him there were a hundred Nereids riding on dolphins, for such was thought to be the number of them by the men of those days. There were also in the interior of the temple other images which had been dedicated by private persons. And around the temple on the outside were placed statues of gold of all the descendants of the ten kings and of their wives, and there were many other great offerings of kings and of private persons, coming both from the city itself and from the foreign cities over which they held sway. There was an altar too, which in size and workmanship corresponded to this magnificence, and the palaces, in like manner, answered to the greatness of the kingdom and the glory of the temple.

In the next place, they had fountains, one of cold and another of hot water, in gracious plenty flowing; and they were wonderfully adapted for use by reason of the pleasantness and excellence of their waters. They constructed buildings about them and planted suitable trees, also they made cisterns, some open to the heavens, others roofed over, to be used in winter as warm baths; there were the kings' baths, and the baths of private persons, which were kept apart; and there were separate baths for women, and for horses and cattle, and to each of them they gave as much adornment as was suitable. Of the water which ran off they carried some to the grove of Poseidon, where were growing all manner of trees of wonderful height and beauty, owing to the excellence of the soil, while the remainder was conveyed by aqueducts along the bridges to the outer circles; and there were many temples built and dedicated to many gods; also gardens and places of exercise, some for men, and others for horses in both of the two islands formed by the zones; and in the centre of the larger of the two there was set apart a race-course of a stadium in width, and in length allowed to extend all round the island, for horses to race in. Also there were guardhouses at intervals for the guards, the more trusted of whom were appointed-to keep watch in the lesser zone, which was nearer the Acropolis while the most trusted of all had houses given them within the citadel, near the persons of the kings. The docks were full of triremes and naval stores, and all things were quite ready for use. Enough of the plan of the royal palace.

Leaving the palace and passing out across the three you came to a wall which began at the sea and went all round: this was everywhere distant fifty stadia from the largest zone or harbour, and enclosed the whole, the ends meeting at the mouth of the channel which led to the sea. The entire area was densely crowded with habitations; and the canal and the largest of the harbours were full of vessels and merchants coming from all parts, who, from their numbers, kept up a multitudinous sound of human voices, and din and clatter of all sorts night and day.

I have described the city and the environs of the ancient palace nearly in the words of Solon, and now I must endeavour to represent the nature and arrangement of the rest of the land. The whole country was said by him to be very lofty and precipitous on the side of the sea, but the country immediately about and surrounding the city was a level plain, itself surrounded by mountains which descended towards the sea; it was smooth and even, and of an oblong shape, extending in one direction three thousand stadia, but across the centre inland it was two thousand stadia. This part of the island looked towards the south, and was sheltered from the north. The surrounding mountains were celebrated for their number and size and beauty, far beyond any which still exist, having in them also many wealthy villages of country folk, and rivers, and lakes, and meadows supplying food enough for every animal, wild or tame, and much wood of various sorts, abundant for each and every kind of work.

I will now describe the plain, as it was fashioned by nature and by the labours of many generations of kings through long ages. It was for the most part rectangular and oblong, and where falling out of the straight line followed the circular ditch. The depth, and width, and length of this ditch were incredible, and gave the impression that a work of such extent, in addition to so many others, could never have been artificial. Nevertheless I must say what I was told. It was excavated to the depth of a hundred, feet, and its breadth was a stadium everywhere; it was carried round the whole of the plain, and was ten thousand stadia in length. It received the streams which came down from the mountains, and winding round the plain and meeting at the city, was there let off into the sea. Further inland, likewise, straight canals of a hundred feet in width were cut from it through the plain, and again let off into the ditch leading to the sea: these canals were at intervals of a hundred stadia, and by them they brought down the wood from the mountains to the city, and conveyed the fruits of the earth in ships, cutting transverse passages from one canal into another, and to the city. Twice in the year they gathered the fruits of the earth—in winter having the benefit of the rains of heaven, and in summer the water which the land supplied by introducing streams from the canals.

As to the population, each of the lots in the plain had to find a leader for the men who were fit for military service, and the size of a lot was a square of ten stadia each way, and the total number of all the lots was sixty thousand. And of the inhabitants of the mountains and of the rest of the country there was also a vast multitude, which was distributed among the lots and had leaders assigned to them according to their districts and villages. The leader was required to furnish for the war the sixth portion of a war-chariot, so as to make up a total of ten thousand chariots; also two horses and riders for them, and a pair of chariot-horses without a seat, accompanied by a horseman who could fight on foot carrying a small shield, and having a charioteer who stood behind the man-at-arms to guide the two horses; also, he was bound to furnish two heavy armed soldiers, two slingers, three stone-shooters and three javelin-men, who were light-armed, and four sailors to make up the complement of twelve hundred ships. Such was the military order of the royal city—the order of the other nine governments varied, and it would be wearisome to recount their several differences.

As to offices and honours, the following was the arrangement from the first. Each of the ten kings in his own division and in his own city had the absolute control of the citizens, and, in most cases, of the laws, punishing and slaying whomsoever he would. Now the order of precedence among them and their mutual relations were regulated by the commands of Poseidon which the law had handed down. These were inscribed by the first kings on a pillar of orichalcum, which was situated in the middle of the island, at the temple of Poseidon, whither the kings were gathered together every fifth and every sixth year alternately, thus giving equal honour to the odd and to the even number. And when they were gathered together they consulted about their common interests, and enquired if any one had transgressed in anything and passed judgment and before they passed judgment they gave their pledges to one another on this wise: There were bulls who had the range of the temple of Poseidon; and the ten kings, being left alone in the temple, after they had offered prayers to the god that they might capture the victim which was acceptable to him, hunted the bulls, without weapons but with staves and nooses; and the bull which they caught they led up to the pillar and cut its throat over the top of it so that the blood fell upon the sacred inscription. Now on the pillar, besides the laws, there was inscribed an oath invoking mighty curses on the disobedient. When therefore, after slaying the bull in the accustomed manner, they had burnt its limbs, they filled a bowl of wine and cast in a clot of blood for each of them; the rest of the victim they put in the fire, after having purified the column all round. Then they drew from the bowl in golden cups and pouring a libation on the fire, they swore that they would judge according to the laws on the pillar, and would punish him who in any point had already transgressed them, and that for the future they would not, if they could help, offend against the writing on the pillar, and would neither command others, nor obey any ruler who commanded them, to act otherwise than according to the laws of their father Poseidon. This was the prayer which each of them offered up for himself and for his descendants, at the same time drinking and dedicating the cup out of which he drank in the temple of the god; and after they had supped and satisfied their needs, when darkness came on, and the fire about the sacrifice was cool, all of them put on most beautiful azure robes, and, sitting on the ground, at night, over the embers of the sacrifices by which they had sworn, and extinguishing all the fire about the temple, they received and gave judgment, if any of them had an accusation to bring against any one; and when they given judgment, at daybreak they wrote down their sentences on a golden tablet, and dedicated it together with their robes to be a memorial.

There were many special laws affecting the several kings inscribed about the temples, but the most important was the following: They were not to take up arms against one another, and they were all to come to the rescue if any one in any of their cities attempted to overthrow the royal house; like their ancestors, they were to deliberate in common about war and other matters, giving the supremacy to the descendants of Atlas. And the king was not to have the power of life and death over any of his kinsmen unless he had the assent of the majority of the ten.

Such was the vast power which the god settled in the lost island of Atlantis; and this he afterwards directed against our land for the following reasons, as tradition tells: For many generations, as long as the divine nature lasted in them, they were obedient to the laws, and well-affectioned towards the god, whose seed they were; for they possessed true and in every way great spirits, uniting gentleness with wisdom in the various chances of life, and in their intercourse with one another. They despised everything but virtue, caring little for their present state of life, and thinking lightly of the possession of gold and other property, which seemed only a burden to them; neither were they intoxicated by luxury; nor did wealth deprive them of their self-control; but they were sober, and saw clearly that all these goods are increased by virtue and friendship with one another, whereas by too great regard and respect for them, they are lost and friendship with them. By such reflections and by the continuance in them of a divine nature, the qualities which we have described grew and increased among them; but when the divine portion began to fade away, and became diluted too often and too much with the mortal admixture, and the human nature got the upper hand, they then, being unable to bear their fortune, behaved unseemly, and to him who had an eye to see grew visibly debased, for they were losing the fairest of their precious gifts; but to those who had no eye to see the true happiness, they appeared glorious and blessed at the very time when they were full of avarice and unrighteous power. Zeus, the god of gods, who rules according to law, and is able to see into such things, perceiving that an honourable race was in a woeful plight, and wanting to inflict punishment on them, that they might be chastened and improve, collected all the gods into their most holy habitation, which, being placed in the centre of the world, beholds all created things. And when he had called them together, he spake as follows. . . ."

(The rest of the Dialogue of Critias was unfinished or has been lost.)

Notes

Chapter 1

1. Herodotus, *The History of Herodotus,* translated from the ancient Greek by George Rawlinson (New York: Tandy-Thomas, 1909), Book I.

2. Ibid., Book II.

3. Plutarch, *Lives,* the Dryden translation edited by Arthur Hugh Clough (New York: Modern Library, 2001), "Solon."

4. A. E. Taylor, *Plato: Timaeus and Critias* (London: Methuen, 1929), 131.

5. Plato, *Timaeus and Critias.* Tr. Desmond Lee (New York: Penguin Books, 1977), *Timaeus* 23b.

6. *Critias,* 120e-121a.

7. *Critias,* 109b-c.

8. *Critias,* 121b.

9. Desmond Lee, *Timaeus and Critias* (New York: Penguin Books, 1977), 165.

10. *Critias,* 120d-e. The Benjamin Jowett translation refers to the Atlanteans as the "seed" of Poseidon.

11. Critias, 116c. ("In the center was a shrine sacred *to* [italic added] Poseidon and Cleito. . . .")

12. *Critias,* 121a-b.

13. *Critias,* 121b-c.

Chapter 2

1. Carl G. Jung and C. Kerényi, *Introduction to a Science of Mythology; the Myth of the Divine Child and the Mysteries of Eleusis,* Tr. by R.F.C. Hull (London: Routledge & Kegan Paul, 1951), 101.

2. Alexander Hislop, *The Two Babylons* (New Jersey: Loizeaux Bros., 2nd Edition, 1959), Chapter III Section II.

3. Barbara G. Walker, *The Woman's Encyclopaedia of Myths and Secrets* (New York: HarperSanFrancisco, 1983), 450.

4. Rufus Camphausen, *The Encyclopaedia of Erotic Wisdom* (Vermont: Inner Traditions International, 1991), 58.

5. Samuel Noah Kramer, *The Sumerians: Their History, Culture and Character* (Chicago: University of Chicago Press, 1963), 117.

6. Stephanie Dalley, *Myths from Mesopotamia: Creation, the Flood, Gilgamesh, and Others.* (Oxford: Oxford University Press, 1989), 15.

7. Thorkild Jacobsen, *The Treasures of Darkness* (New Haven: Yale University Press, 1976), 85.

8. E.A. Wallis Budge, *Osiris and the Egyptian Resurrection* (London: The Medici Society Ltd., 1911), 16.

9. James G. Frazer, *Adonis, Attis, Osiris: Studies in the History of Oriental Religion* (London: Macmillan and Company, 1907), Vol. II, 7.

10. Walker, 453.

11. Franz Cumont, *The Mysteries of Mithra* (New York: Dover Publications, 1956, 1903), 137.

12. Anne Baring and Jules Cashford, *The Myth of the Goddess: Evolution of an Image* (London: Penguin Books, 1993), 395.

13. Walker, 201.

14. Samuel Noah Kramer. *History Begins at Sumer* (Garden City, N.Y.: Doubleday Anchor Books, 1959), 143-144.

15. Theodore Ziolkowski, *The Sin of Knowledge: Ancient Themes and Modern Variations* (New Jersey: Princeton University Press, 2000), 16.

16. "Adam and Eve," *Encyclopaedia Britannica*.

17. Ignatius Donnelly, *Atlantis: The Antediluvian* World (New York: Dover Publications, 1976, c. 1882), 1-2.

Chapter 3

1. *Critias,* 118a.

2. Some of Plato's statements in the *Critias* may give us useful clues about the likely elevation of the highest mountains on Atlantis. If the mountains were the principal source of water for the island, as Plato seems to suggest, they must have had sufficient elevation to cause up-sloping moist air to condense and precipitate over the highlands, putting the leeward slopes in the so-called rain shadow, and consequently leaving the lowlands with less direct precipitation. Warm ocean air at 20°C, for example, when pushed by prevailing winds over high elevations, will typically become supersaturated and begin to condense at around 7°C. A number of seasonal and geographic variables come into play here, but on average, in a temperate zone summer season for instance, the air temperature will reach 7°C at about 2,000 meters. Estimating the mean elevation of the landmass is more difficult, but certainly a significant portion of Atlantis must have risen to at least 5,000 to 7,000 feet.

3. *Timaeus,* 25d.

Chapter 3 continued

4. H.S. Bellamy, *The Atlantis Myth* (London: Faber and Faber, 1948), 85.

5. *Timaeus,* 25a.

6. *Critias,* 113c.

7. *Critias,* 117e.

8. *Critias,* 118a-b.

9. The specific reference to the "cold northerly winds" is found in A.E. Taylor's translation of the *Critias.*

10. Although the island is correctly shown in an elongated form, the Plain of Atlantis should not be at its tip but rather stretch "midway along its greatest length."

11. *Critias,* 118c-d.

12. Other translations of the *Critias* call the Acropolis Hill "a mountain not very high on any side" and "a mountain that was nowhere of any great altitude." See the Benjamin Jowett and the A. E. Taylor translations respectively.

13. *Critias,* 116c-e.

14. *Critias,* 113d-e.

15. Donnelly, 288.

16. *Critias,* 113e.

17. *Timaeus,* 24e-25a.

18. Eberhard Zangger, *The Flood from Heaven: Deciphering the Atlantis Legend* (New York: William Morrow, 1992), 108-111.

19. John Michell, *The Dimension of Paradise: The Proportions and Symbolic Numbers of Ancient Cosmology,* (London: Thames and Hudson, 1988), 134.

Chapter 4

1. Donnelly, 24.

2. Ibid., 328.

3. Karen Pandell with Barry Bryant, *Learning from the Dalai Lama: Secrets of the Wheel of Time* (New York: Dutton Children's Books, 1995).

4. Ibid.

5. Henri Frankfort, *Birth of Civilization in the Near East* (Bloomington: Indiana University Press, 1959), 95.

6. The Frieze depicts Athena and Hephaestus as the champions and protectors of Athens. According to the myth, Hephaestus spilled his seed on the earth and mixed it with dust, from which sprang mankind.

Chapter 4 continued

7. Nigel Pennick, *Hitler's Secret Sciences: His Quest for the Hidden Knowledge of the Ancients* (Neville Spearman, 1981), 104–105.

8. Walker, 965.

9. Thomas Wilson, Curator, Department of Prehistoric Anthropology, U.S. National Museum, *The Swastika, the earliest known symbol, and its migrations with observations on the migration of certain industries in prehistoric times* (Washington, D.C.: Smithsonian Institution Report, 1894), 3–5.

Chapter 5

1. Donnelly, 43.

2. Quote from Ellis, 21.

3. Rodney Castleden, *Atlantis Destroyed* (London: Routledge, 1998), 187.

4. *Timaeus,* 25a. "… from it (Atlantis) travellers could in those days reach the other islands, and from them the whole opposite continent which surrounds what can truly be called the ocean."

5. Collins, 310.

6. Robert Ferro and Michael Grumley, *Atlantis: The Autobiography of a Search* (New York, Bell Publishing, 1970), 34–35.

7. Quote from Ellis, 76.

8. Charles H. Hapgood, *Earth's Shifting Crust: A Key to Some Basic Problems of Earth Science* (New York: Pantheon Books, 1958), 1.

9. Graham Hancock, *Fingerprints of the Gods* (New York: Crown Publishers, 1995), 10.

10. *Critias,* 113a–b.

11. Castleden, 137–138.

12. Charles Pellegrino, *Unearthing Atlantis: An Archaeological Odyssey* (New York: Random House, 1991), 232.

13. Donnelly, 176–177.

14. Zdenek Kukal, *Atlantis: In the Light of Modern Research* (New York: Elsevier, 1984), 191.

15. Kukal, 189.

16. Davis A. Young, *The Biblical Flood* (Grand Rapids: Eerdmans, 1995), 11.

17. Desmond Lee, *Plato: Timaeus and Critias* (New York : Penguin Books, 1977). The Atlantis researchers, according to Lee, belonged to three camps: the crazy, the geological, and the historical. He assigned

the theosophists and occultists in the first group, as well as such distinguished writers as Ignatius Donnelly, saying that for the most part their interpretations are "naively crazy" and that their suggested locations for Atlantis have often nothing to do with Plato's text. The geographical researchers were next on the list, assigned to a more reasonable and scientifically oriented crowd that nonetheless had to stretch the imagination, as well as Plato's story, in order to point to places like the mid-Atlantic ridge and the possible land bridge that supposedly once connected it to Europe. Lewis Spence, Galanopoulos and even Sir Francis Bacon were all assigned to this group of Atlantologists as being "quite capable of their own flights of fancy." The third group he termed the historical researchers, who base their speculations on historical narratives and their solid faith in Plato's integrity. He concluded his remarks on *Timaeus* and *Critias* by stating that if Atlantis was not connected with the destruction of Thera, then perhaps it was a form of "escapism" on the part of the old philosopher, who projected his utopian ideals to some mythical period in the past. In light of the evidence we have put together thus far however, this sentiment seems to represent a rather one-sided and poorly supported opinion.

18. Lee, 158-159.
19. A. G. Galanopoulos, *Atlantis: the truth behind the legend* (Indianapolis: Bobbs-Merrill, 1969).
20. *Timaeus,* 23d-24a.
21. Michell, *The Dimensions of Paradise,* 107.

Chapter 6

1. *Timaeus,* 25d.
2. Donnelly, 36.
3. Bellamy, 78.
4. MacKenzie, 1999; McInnis, 1999
5. Kenneth J. Hsu, *The Mediterranean Was a Desert: A Voyage of the Glomar Challenger* (New Jersey: Princeton University Press, 1983).
6. William Ryan and Walter Pitman, *Noah's Flood: The New Scientific Discoveries about the Event That Changed History* (New York: Simon & Schuster, 1999).

7. According to a National Geographic report on this research, as the glaciers began to melt at the end of the Ice Age some 12,000 years ago, eventually "a wall of seawater surged from the Mediterranean into the Black Sea." The coastal farms of the Black Sea were hit with a tremendous force and the terrified survivors perpetuated the story, which they suggest "was passed down through the generations and eventually became the Noah story."

8. Ryan and Pitman, 75.

9. Hsu, *The Mediterranean Was a Desert,* 163. ". . . but we now had evidence that there had been a deep sea in the Mediterranean between episodes of desiccation."

10. Ibid., 101.

11. Ryan and Pitman, 81.

12. At the same time, there is a heightened frequency of earthquakes— generated as vibrations are transmitted through hundreds of miles of continental granite, thus causing the whole Mediterranean rim to reverberate like a giant, crudely constructed tuning fork. If the analogy holds, it is easy to see how the eastern Mediterranean might be especially unstable, being situated at the 'focus' or curved end of the fork.

13. Ryan and Pitman, 147.

14. Ibid., 89.

15. Hsu, *The Mediterranean Was a Desert,* 177.

16. Kenneth J. Hsu, *Challenger at Sea: A Ship That Revolutionized Earth Science* (New Jersey: Princeton University Press, 1992), 269.

17. Hsu, *The Mediterranean Was a Desert,* 176.

18. Ibid., 171.

19. Ryan and Pitman, 85.

20. Charles Berlitz, *The Mystery of Atlantis* (New York: Grosset & Dunlap, 1969), 45.

21. Ryan and Pitman, 96.

22. Hsu, *The Mediterranean Was a Desert,* 101.

23. H.G. Wells, *The Outline of History* (New York: The Macmillan Company, 1921), 90-91.

24. "Mediterranean Sea," *Encyclopaedia Britannica.*

Chapter 7

1. *Critias,* 115d-116a.

2. J. K. Hall and A. Valery, editors, *Geological Structure of the North-Eastern Mediterranean,* (Historical Productions-Hall, Jerusalem, 1994), 307.

3. Donnelly, 304.

4. Stass Paraskos, *Aphrodite Cypris, Goddess of Love: The Mythology of Cyprus* (England: Interworld Publications, 1988), 12.

5. Ibid., 17.

6. Satellites are sometimes used to gather general information about the seafloor (altimetry), but the resulting data is comparatively poor.

7. Hall, 2.

8. Ibid., 7.

9. The Scotia Group, Inc., is based in Dallas, Texas (www.Scotia-group.com).

10. The three dimensional images of the eastern Mediterranean seafloor and Cyprus's topography, with their vibrant color, clarity and effective rendering of light and perspective were produced with the Visualization Tool Kit (VTK; www.kitware.com). The elevation data was obtained from the National Oceanic and Atmospheric Administration (NOAA) web site www.ngdc.noaa.gov), and the shoreline data was obtained from the USGS web site (http://crusty.er.usgs.gov/coast/getcoast.html). Creation of the structured point data sets from the irregular bathymetric data was done with an iterative, convergent gridding process, used for computer-aided mapping. Data management, processing and programming to create the images was done on a PC platform using commercially available and public domain software by Patrick Lowry at The Scotia Group, Inc.

11. A connection to be made in this regard, and one which supports the general thesis of this study, can be found in a somewhat unusual source known as the *Urantia Book.* Its account of the Garden of Eden—the way it appeared and how it was structured—contains a number of similarities to Plato's account of Atlantis. Eden is described as a "long and narrow" peninsula stretching westward from the eastern shores of the Mediterranean Sea, with a 27-mile long neck attaching it to the eastern mainland. Also mentioned is a "great river" that went out from the peninsula onto the mainland, as well as a "central sector" in the middle of the Garden that was surrounded by four quadrants where the Adamites built universities, temples, administrative centers, and residential quarters. Although the general description is very similar to Plato's

Atlantis, the mention of the 27-mile neck and the location of the peninsula in the eastern Mediterranean vicinity is unique to the *Urantia Book*. It also reports that the peninsula sank beneath the sea in connection with natural processes resulting from the destruction of the Gibraltar dam. Proving the validity of the *Urantia Book* is beyond the scope of our investigation. It is mentioned here because its account is so highly correlative with our inferences and empirical data pointing to the eastern Mediterranean as the place to look for the lost civilization Plato described as Atlantis.

Chapter 8

1. The main rivers of southeastern Turkey are the Seyhan, Ceyhan, and Goksu, which presently flow into the Mediterranean Sea. The average annual flows of the Seyhan and the Ceyhan Rivers are respectively, 3.959 and 2.777 billion CM, allowing Turkey to export the large volume of water from these rivers to neighboring countries.
2. Hall, 113.
3. Ibid., 129. ". . . later, Eratosthenes Seamount was again submerged."
4. Ibid., 395.
5. "Cyprus," *Encyclopaedia Britannica*.
6. *Critias*, 118c-e.
7. *Critias*, 118b.
8. Donnelly, 324.
9. Ibid., 288.
10. *Critias*, 118c-e.
11. "Cyprus," *Encyclopaedia Britannica*.
12. *Critias*, 15a.
13. Frazer, 7.
14. *Critias*, 118e.
15. Donnelly, 246.
16. "Padmasambhava's Copper Mountain Paradise," *Ohio State University, Department of History of Art*.
17. Kukal, 191.
18. "Copper processing," *Encyclopaedia Britannica*.
19. Donnelly, 326.
20. Ibid., 216.
21. Ibid., 253.

Select Bibliography

Baring, Anne and Jules Cashford. *The Myth of the Goddess: Evolution of an Image.* London: Penguin Books, 1993.

Bellamy, H.S. *The Atlantis Myth.* London: Faber and Faber Ltd., 1948.

Berlitz, Charles. *Atlantis: The Eighth Continent.* New York: G.P. Putnam's, 1984.

Berlitz, Charles. *The Mystery of Atlantis.* New York: Grosset & Dunlap, 1969.

Binger, Tilde. *Asherah, Goddesses in Ugarit, Israel and the Old Testament.* England: Sheffield Academic Press, 1997.

Budge, Wallis. *Osiris and the Egyptian Resurrection.* London: The Medici Society, 1911.

Bullfinch, Thomas. *The Age of Fable.* Philadelphia: David McKay, 1898.

Campbell, Joseph. *The Masks of God: Creative Mythology.* New York: Arkana, 1968.

Camphausen, Rufus. *The Encyclopaedia of Erotic Wisdom.* Vermont: Inner Traditions International, 1991.

Castleden, Rodney. *Atlantis Destroyed.* London: Routledge, 1998.

Childress, David Hatcher. *Lost Cities of Atlantis, Ancient Europe & the Mediterranean.* Stelle: Adventures Unlimited Press, 1996.

Cott, Jonathan. *Isis and Osiris: Exploring the Goddess Myth.* New York: Doubleday, 1994.

Cumont, Franz. *The Mysteries of Mithra.* New York: Dover Publications, 1956, 1903.

Dalley, Stephanie. *Myths from Mesopotamia: Creation, the Flood, Gilgamesh, and Others.* Oxford: Oxford University Press, 1989.

Davis, John D. *Genesis and Semitic Tradition.* New York: Charles Scribner's Sons, 1894.

Donnelly, Ignatius. *Atlantis: The Antediluvian World.* New York: Dover Publications, 1976.

Ferro, Robert and Michael Grumley. *Atlantis: The Autobiography of a Search.* New York: Bell Publishing, 1970.

Forsyth, Phyllis Young. *Atlantis: The Making of a Myth.* Montreal: McGill-Queen's University Press, 1980.

Frankfort, Henri. *Birth of Civilization in the Near East.* Bloomington: Indiana University Press, 1959.

Frazer, James G. *Adonis, Attis, Osiris: Studies in the History of Oriental Religion.* London: Macmillan and Co., 1907.

Galanopoulos, A. G. *Atlantis: the truth behind the legend.* Indianapolis: Bobbs–Merrill, 1969.

Goodrick-Clarke, Nicholas. *Black Sun: Aryan Cults, Esoteric Nazism and the Politics of Identity.* New York: New York University Press, 2002.

Gray, Louis H., editor. *The Mythology of All Races.* Boston: Marshal Jones Company, 1916.

Griffiths, Gwyn J. *The Origins of Osiris and His Cult.* Leiden: E.J. Brill, 1980.

Grigson, Geoffrey. *The Goddess of Love: The Birth, Triumph, Death and Return of Aphrodite.* England: Constable and Company Limited, 1976.

Handcock, Percy Stuart Peache. *Mesopotamian Archaeology: An Introduction to the Archaeology of Babylonia and Assyria.* New York: Putnam, 1912.

Hall, J. K. and A. Valery, editors. *Geological Structure of the North-Eastern Mediterranean.* Historical Productions-Hall, Jerusalem, 1994.

Hapgood, Charles H. *Earth's Shifting Crust: A Key to Some Basic Problems of Earth Science.* New York: Pantheon Books, 1958.

Heidel, Alexander. *The Gilgamesh Epic and Old Testament Parallels.* Chicago: University of Chicago Press, 1963.

Hislop, Alexander. *The Two Babylons.* New Jersey: Loizeaux Bros., 1959.

Hsu, Kenneth J. *The Mediterranean Was a Desert: A Voyage of the Glomar Challenger.* New Jersey: Princeton University Press, 1983.

Jacobsen, Thorkild. *The Treasures of Darkness.* New Haven: Yale University Press, 1976.

Jung, Carl G. and C. Kerényi. *Introduction to a Science of Mythology; the Myth of the Divine Child and the Mysteries of Eleusis,* Tr. by R.F.C. Hull. London: Routledge & Kegan Paul, 1951.

Kramer, Samuel Noah. *History Begins at Sumer.* New York: Doubleday Anchor Books, 1959.

Kramer, Samuel Noah. *The Sumerians: Their History, Culture and Character.* Chicago: University of Chicago Press, 1963.

Kramer, Samuel Noah and J. Maier. *Myths of Enki, the Crafty God.* New York/Oxford: Oxford University Press, 1989.

Kukal, Zdenek. *Atlantis: In the Light of Modern Research*. New York: Elsevier, 1984.

Lane, Eugene N., editor. *Cybele, Attis and Related Cults: Essays in Memory of M.J. Vermaseren*. New York: E.J. Brill, 1996.

Layard, Henry. *Nineveh and Babylon: A Narrative of a Second Expedition to Assyria During the Years 1849, 1850, & 1851*. London: J. Murray, 1882 [pref. 1867].

Mackenzie, Donald A. *Myths of Babylonia and Assyria*. London: Gresham Publishing Company Ltd., 1915.

Mendelsohn, Isaac. *Religions of the Ancient Near East: Sumero-Akkadian Religious Texts and Ugaritic Epics*. New York: Liberal Arts Press, 1955.

Mitchell, John. *The Dimension of Paradise: The Proportions and Symbolic Numbers of Ancient Cosmology*. London: Thames and Hudson, 1988.

Narby, Jeremy. *The Cosmic Serpent: DNA and the Origins of Knowledge*. New York: Jeremy P. Tarcher/Putnam, 1998.

Olschak, Blanche C. and Geshe T. Wangyal, *Mystic Art of Ancient Tibet*. Boston: Shambhala, 1987.

Page, Hugh. *The Myth of Cosmic Rebellion*. The Netherlands: E.J. Brill, Leiden, 1996.

Paraskos, Stass. *Aphrodite Cypris, Goddess of Love: The Mythology of Cyprus*. England: Interworld Publications, 1988.

Pellegrino, Charles. *Unearthing Atlantis: An Archaeological Odyssey*. New York: Random House, 1991.

Plato. *Timaeus and Critias*. Tr. Desmond Lee. New York: Penguin Books, 1977.

Plato. *Timaeus and Critias*. Tr. A. E Taylor. London: Methuen, 1929.

Pritchard, James Bennett. *Ancient Near Eastern Texts Relating to the Old Testament*. New Jersey: Princeton University Press, 1955.

Rogers, Robert William. *A History of Ancient Persia*. New York: Charles Scribner's Sons, 1929.

Ryan, William and Walter Pitman. *Noah's Flood: The New Scientific Discoveries about the Event That Changed History*. New York: Simon & Schuster, 1999.

Sayce, Archibald H. *Religions of Ancient Egypt and Babylonia*. New York: AMS Press, 1979, 1903.

Showerman, Grant. *The Great Mother of the Gods*. University of Wisconsin, 1901.

Sitchin, Zecharia. *The 12th Planet*. New York: Avon Books, 1978.

Spanuth, Jurgen. *Atlantis of the North*. London: Sidgwick & Jackson, 1979.

Spence, Lewis. *Myths and Legends of Babylonia and Assyria*. Boston: David D. Nickerson, 1915.

The Urantia Book. Chicago: The Urantia Foundation, 1955.

Walker, Barbara G. *The Woman's Encyclopedia of Myths and Secrets*. New York: HarperSanFrancisco, 1983.

Walls, Neal H. *The Goddess Anat in Ugaritic Myth*. Georgia: Scholars Press, 1922.

Wells, H.G. *The Outline of History*. New York: The Macmillan Company, 1921.

Wolkstein, Diane and Samuel N. Kramer. *Inanna, Queen of Heaven and Earth: Her Stories and Hymns from Sumer*. New York: Harper & Row Publishers, 1983.

Wynne-Tyson, Esme. *Mithras: The Fellow in the Cap*. England: Centaur Press Ltd., 1972, 1958.

Young, Davis A. *The Biblical Flood*. Grand Rapids: Eerdmans, 1995.

Zangger, Eberhard. *The Flood from Heaven: Deciphering the Atlantis Legend*. New York: William Morrow, 1992.

Ziolkowski, Theodore. *The Sin of Knowledge: Ancient Themes and Modern Variations*. New Jersey: Princeton University Press, 2000.

Picture Credits

Chapter 1

1:1 Courtesy of the Architect of the Capitol, Washington, D.C.

1:2 André Thevet, *Les Vrais Pourtraits et Vies Hommes Illustres,* 1584 edition supplied by the Special Collections Library, University of Michigan.

1:3 Architect of the Capitol, Washington, D.C.

Chapter 2

2:1 Spence, Lewis. *Myths and Legends of Babylonia and Assyria.* Boston: David D. Nickerson, 1915.

Chapter 3

3:1 *New York American,* October 20, 1912.

3:2 Courtesy of Bo Atkinson.

3:3 Bo Atkinson.

3:4 Illustration by Robert Sarmast.

3:5 Robert Sarmast, copyright 2003.

3:6 Robert Sarmast.

Chapter 4

4:1 Library of Congress, Prints and Photographs Division [reproduction number, LC-USZ62-78860].

4:2 Library of Congress, [reproduction number, LC-USZ62-122902].

4:3 Courtesy of the National Oceanic and Atmospheric Administration (NOAA), U.S. Department of Commerce.

4:4 NOAA.

4:5 Library of Congress, Prints and Photographs Division [reproduction number, LC-USZC2-3405].

4:6 Architect of the Capitol, Washington, D.C.

Chapter 5

5:1 Courtesy of the University of Texas at Austin, Perry-Castañeda Library Map Collection.

5:2 NOAA.

5:3 NOAA.

5:4 University of Texas at Austin.

5:5   NOAA.

5.6   University of Texas at Austin.

5:7   National Aeronautic and Space Administration (NASA).

5:8   NOAA.

5:9   NASA.

5:10 NOAA.

Chapter 6

6:1   NOAA, outline by R. Sarmast.

6:2   NASA.

6:3   NOAA.

6:4   Gustav Dore.

Chapter 7

7:1   NASA.

7:2   NASA.

7:3   Courtesy of Freydoon Rassouli (http://www.rassouli.com).

7:4   Courtesy of Dr. John K. Hall, Geological Survey of Israel.

7:5   NOAA, outline by R. Sarmast.

7:6   Dr. John K. Hall.

7:7   Dr. John K. Hall.

7:8   Dr. John K. Hall.

Chapter 8

8:1   Robert Sarmast.

8:2 – 8.8 Robert Sarmast.

8:9   NOAA.

8:10 Robert Sarmast.

8:11 *New York American,* October 20, 1912.

8:12 – 8:21 Robert Sarmast.

Epilogue

E:1   Bo Atkinson.

Index

A

Abel · 25
Acropolis · 33, 37, 38, 39, 46, 48, 50,
    51, 54, 55, 56, 59, 60, 61, 115,
    120, 147, 149, 150, 151, 152, 153,
    162, 164
Adana · 135
Adonis · 21, 119, 121
Aegean Sea · 45, 46, 74, 87, 88
Africa · 49, 73, 80, 81, 84, 85, 98, 99,
    101, 105, 106, 110, 119, 140, 143
Antarctica · 44, 65, 76, 77, 78, 79, 85
Aphrodite · 59, 117, 119, 120, 121
Arabia · 17, 26, 54, 110, 142
Aristotle · 2, 6, 64
Artemis · 17
Aryan · 22, 57, 58
Asia · 45, 46, 49, 80, 84, 85, 107,
    119, 143
Assyrians · 107, 156
Athena · 55
Athens · 3, 6, 8, 55, 92
Atlantean · 10, 11, 13, 18, 19, 21, 29,
    34, 37, 39, 49, 50, 53, 57, 58, 63,
    67, 76, 80, 82, 84, 85, 92, 96, 112,
    119, 143, 154, 165
Atlanteans · 12, 13, 19, 20, 24, 31,
    35, 40, 42, 48, 58, 75, 86, 97, 109,
    115, 142, 155, 156, 160
Atlantic · 5, 6, 45, 66, 67, 69, 70, 71,
    75, 80, 81, 82, 83, 84, 85, 86, 91,
    99, 100, 101, 104, 105, 106, 109,
    133, 164
Atlantis City · 29, 31, 32, 33, 37, 38,
    39, 40, 47, 48, 59, 120, 144, 149,
    152, 153, 155
Atlantis Proper · 32
Atlas · 32, 37
Atrahasis · 19

Attis · 21, 22
Azores · 65, 66, 67, 69, 70, 71, 72, 74

B

Baal · 160
Babylonians · 17, 107
Bahamas · 71, 72, 73, 74, 85
Bermuda · 65
Bible · 23, 24, 25
Biblical · 26, 27, 112, 161
Bimini · 65, 72, 73, 74, 75
Black Sea · 45, 108
Bolivia · 65, 75, 76, 82, 85
Bosporus · 45
Brumidi, Constantino · 14, 62
Buddhist · 54, 155

C

Cain · 25, 26
Campbell, Joseph · 16, 20
Canary Islands · 65, 67, 71
Capitol · 3, 59, 60
Caribbean · 72, 73
Catholic · 54
Cayce, Edgar · 72, 73
Christian · 5, 8, 51, 54, 17
Christianity · 121
Cilicia Basin · 135
Columbus · 71, 100
Crantor · 7
Cretans · 86, 96, 97, 109
Crete · 56, 65, 83, 84, 87, 88, 106,
    140
Critias · 1, 2, 3, 6, 8, 9, 11, 19, 20, 28,
    29, 33, 42, 43, 47, 51, 56, 70, 80,
    81, 82, 83, 87, 91, 95, 96, 108,
    115, 138, 140, 144, 147, 150, 152

Cross of Atlantis · 51

Cuba · 65

Cybele · 22

Cyprus · 17, 51, 52, 83, 96, 102, 106,
112, 113, 115, 117, 118, 119, 120,
121, 122, 123, 125, 127, 128, 130,
131, 133, 134, 135, 136, 137, 138,
139, 140, 141, 142, 143, 144, 147,
148, 152, 153, 154, 155, 156, 158,
162

Cyprus Arc · 125, 131, 133, 134, 135,
140, 142, 144, 148, 153

D

Dardanelles · 45

Deucalion · 26

Diana · 17, 18

Dome of the Rock, · 54

Donnelly, Ignatius · 26, 51, 67, 70,
85, 98, 119, 146, 155, 157, 160,
162

E

Earthquakes · 67, 87, 97, 98, 100,
112, 140

Eden · 15, 26, 157, 158, 159, 163

Egypt · 3, 4, 5, 6, 7, 9, 12, 15, 20, 21,
32, 45, 54, 55, 76, 84, 92, 97, 105,
119, 141, 161

Egyptian · 4, 7, 9, 10, 11, 13, 17, 18,
20, 21, 22, 32, 44, 45, 47, 56, 57,
72, 82, 83, 87, 92, 96, 100, 109,
160

Elephants · 42, 43, 49, 106, 156, 157

Enki · 18, 19, 20, 22

Enlil · 19

Ephesian · 17

Eratosthenes Seamount · 140

Euphrates · 17, 19, 160

Eurasia · 99, 142

Europe · 45, 49, 80, 81, 85, 97, 98,
101, 105, 119, 140, 143, 155

European · 58, 66, 69, 104, 105

Eve · 26

F

Flood · 23, 30, 45, 86, 99, 103, 121

G

Garden of Eden · 26, 28, 51, 157

Gardens of the Hesperides · 26, 39,
146

Genesis · 23, 25, 108, 157, 158

Germany · 65, 123

Giants · 11, 15, 23, 24

Gilgamesh · 19, 24, 25, 108

Glomar Challenger · 102, 103, 107

Goddess · 8, 9, 17, 21, 22, 62

Golden Age · 2, 8, 15, 42, 163

Graham Island · 98, 99

Greece · 3, 4, 9, 15, 54, 63, 84, 86,
107, 119, 141, 161

Greek · 3, 4, 7, 9, 10, 22, 23, 31, 39,
44, 45, 47, 55, 65, 82, 83, 86, 89,
119, 145, 146, 160

Greeks · 4, 5, 9, 11, 13, 18, 26, 156,
160

H

H.M.S. Challenger · 67, 68

Hall, John K. · 118, 122, 123, 125,
126, 141

Hanging Gardens · 54

Hebrew · 25, 160

Hecataeus · 45

Hephaestus · 60

Herodotus · 3, 4

Hindu · 53, 155

Hitler · 57, 58

Horus · 21

Hsu, Kenneth J. · 99, 102, 104, 105,
106, 107, 108, 111

I

India · 15, 26, 52, 54, 58, 71

Iranian · 22

Iraq · 24

Ishtar · 17, 18
Isis · 18, 20, 21, 154
Islamic · 7, 17, 26, 54
Israel · 25, 123, 146
Italy · 107

J

Jefferson, Thomas · 14
Jung, Carl · 16
Jupiter · 6, 17

K

Kabir River · 158, 159
Karpas Peninsula · 144
Kataklysmos · 121
Keftiu · 83

L

Land of Nod · 26
Latakia · 135, 158, 160
Lebanon · 146, 158
Lee, Desmond · 11, 87
Levantine Basin · 121, 125, 140

M

Magi · 92
Magnesia · 56
Mandala · 52, 53
Manetho · 7
Manu · 26
Mecca · 54
Mercury · 60
Mesopotamia · 15, 21, 54, 119
Mesopotamian · 19, 21, 22, 25, 54
Middle East · 25, 65, 81
Minerva · 55, 59, 62
Minoan · 75, 84, 87, 88, 90
Mithra · 18, 22
Mithraism · 22
Morocco · 100
Mother Goddess · 21

Mt. Parnassus · 26
Mt. Meru · 55
Muhammad · 17

N

Nazi · 57, 58
Near East · 54, 80, 117
Neptune · 59
New Testament · 17
Nile · 9, 105, 106
Noah · 18, 24, 26, 103, 108
North America · 72

O

Obelisk · 56, 57
Old Testament · 157
Olympian · 9, 119
Olympus · 117, 120, 139, 142, 144, 158
Orontes River · 159
Osiris · 18, 20, 21, 22, 154

P

Pacific Ocean · 75
Palestine · 25, 119
Paphos · 117, 119
Paradise · 15, 19, 22, 26, 29, 46, 51, 121, 155
Parthenon · 55, 56
Pentecost, Day of · 121
Persian · 18, 22, 52, 53, 92
Persians · 18, 22, 107, 156
Philo · 86
Phoenicia · 92
Phoenician · 82
Phoenicians · 156, 160
Pillars of Heracles · 45, 86
Pillars of Hercules · 45, 66, 72, 91
Pitman, Walter · 103, 108
Plutarch · 5, 6, 20, 128
Poseidon · 10, 12, 13, 14, 19, 22, 32, 37, 38, 43, 59, 62, 119, 155

Proclus · 6, 7
Pyramids · 53, 54, 55

R

Rhodes · 140
Rock of Gibraltar · 82
Romans · 18, 119, 156, 160
Rome · 17, 22, 54, 56, 57, 63, 119
Russia · 123
Ryan, William · 102, 103, 104, 106, 108, 111

S

Santorini · 88, 89, 90, 91
Schliemann, Heinrich · 34
Sicily · 98
Socrates · 1, 2, 8, 9
Solon · 3, 4, **5**, 7, 9, 11, 12, 29, 45, 72, 80, 82, 84, 87, 91, 92, 100, 109, 128, 150
Sonchis · 5
Sons of God · 23
South America · 44, 54, 72, 75, 76, 80
Spain · 65, 84, 98, 100, 106
St. Peter's Square · 57
Statue of Liberty · 61
Strabo · 6, 95
Strait of Gibraltar · 45, 66, 67, 71, 72, 80, 81, 99, 100, 101, 104, 105
Sumerian · 18, 19, 20, 25, 63, 157
Sumerians · 9, 18, 19, 20, 25, 54
Swastika · 58
Syria · 121, 123, 130, 131, 136, 144, 146, 147, 158, 160
Syrian · 17, 144, 158, 159

T

Taurus · 135
Tectonic plates · 30, 70, 79, 99, 142
Temple Mount · 54
Thera · 65, 75, 87, 88, 89, 90, 91, 92
Thoth · 7

Thule Society · 57
Tibet · 52
Tigris River · 19
Timaeus · 1, 2, 8, 9, 29, 31, 45, 46, 47, 83, 92, 95, 96, 108
Tree of Life · 24, 54, 157
Troodos Massif · 139, 142, 158
Troy · 34, 65
Tsunami · 30, 70, 90
Turkey · 84, 119, 134, 135, 146

U

Ugarit · 160

V

Vatican · 56
Venus · 14, 17, 59, 119
Volcanic · 30, 43, 49, 67, 76, 79, 88, 90, 91, 112, 143
Volcanoes · 43, 70, 87, 98, 140
Vulcan · 60

W

West Tartus Ridge · 136, 158
Wells, H.G. · 109, 112

Z

Zeus · 12, 13, 23, 24, 26
Ziggurats · 54, 55

CYPRUS ATLANTIS

EXPEDITION 2004

For full-color maps,
3D models, animation files,
and to receive updates,
go to:

www.DiscoveryofAtlantis.com

About the Author:

Robert Sarmast is a writer and explorer who
has traveled the world in search of clues for
solving some of the world's most enduring
mysteries. His research over the last fifteen
years has targeted the location of Atlantis and
uncovered groundbreaking evidence first
reported in his book *Discovery of Atlantis:
The Startling Case for the Island of Cyprus*,
published in 2003, and now updated in
this expanded edition.

In 2004 he founded First Source Enterprises,
LLC, to promote more extensive research in
this area, which led to the world's first scientific
Atlantis expedition and yielded sufficient
evidence to ignite a global sensation. He is
the leader of the Cyprus-Atlantis Project and
currently resides on the island of Cyprus
where he is organizing a second underwater
expedition that will include a documentary
film series about this extraordinary discovery.